SHAKESPEARE'S COMEDIES

Shakespeare's Comedies

Explorations in Form

By Ralph Berry

Princeton University Press, Princeton, N. J.

References are to the Pelican Edition of Shakespeare, ed. Alfred Harbage (Baltimore, Maryland, 1969). Statistics of word-frequencies are taken from Martin Spevack, *A Complete and Systematic Concordance to the Works of Shakespeare*, 3 vols. (Hildesheim, West Germany, 1968).

Chapter IV, "The Words of Mercury," was first published in *Shakespeare Survey 22*, 1970, Cambridge University Press, Cambridge, England.

Chapter VI, "The Merchant of Venice," incorporates material first published in *Studia Anglica Posnaniensia IV*, 1972, Poznań, Poland.

Chapter VIII, "Problems of Knowing," was first published in *English Studies*, 1971, Swets & Zeitlinger N.V., Lisse, The Netherlands.

Chapter IX, "No Exit from Arden," was first published in *Modern Language Review*, 1971, Modern Humanities Research Association, University of Birmingham, Birmingham, England.

The author wishes to thank the editors and publishers for their permission to reprint, in a somewhat revised form, material which originally appeared in their journals; and the University of Manitoba, for a grant towards secretarial assistance in the preparation of the manuscript.

This book has been set in Linotype Times Roman

Printed in the United States of America

by Princeton University Press, Princeton, New Jersey

FOR MARCUS

Contents

SHAKESPEARE'S COMEDIES

Introduction

Two major courses are open to the writer on the comedies of Shakespeare. One is to treat of Shakespeare's comedies; and the other, of Shakespearean comedy. The decision taken is usually apparent in the book's title. Not invariably: for some, "Shakespearean comedy" is simply a loose, collective noun for Shakespeare's comedies. There is no, as it were, ideological commitment. Generally, however, "Shakespearean comedy" implies the view that some kind of comic structure is common to all his comedies, and that this structure can be elicited and described. Those holding the alternative view formally disclaim, through "Shakespeare's comedies," so ambitious an enterprise.

This study is concerned solely with comedies. It has no larger aspirations, and the reasons will bear elaboration. Manifestly, the difficulties of synthesizing some 15 to 16 comedies into a single comic structure are very great, for the broad category contains plays that are quite unlike. They belong, in effect, to separate species. One usually speaks of the farces, the problem comedies, and the final romances, in addition to the main wave of Shakespeare's comedies that ends with *Twelfth Night*. But if one believes in Shakespearean comedy, one cannot stop there; the demarcation line is quite unreal. So

3

one has to weigh the implications of the comic matter in the plays that are not comedies. This line of enquiry can begin with the Falstaff scenes in *Henry IV*; and that implies a view of history. It may end with the questions posed by Wilson Knight, who discerns the contours of a grotesque comedy embedded in the agony of *King Lear*; and that involves a view of tragedy. All this constitutes a sufficiently formidable challenge to theory. More than that, the quest for Shakespearean comedy involves, I find, a more practical objection. It is an old story. The edifice of Shakespearean comedy must largely be built out of Shakespeare's comedies; and the units come in a wide variety of shapes. They are moreover somewhat irregular in form. So the theoretician-architect finds that the stability of his edifice will be enormously increased if he can regularize his building materials. That, unfortunately, leads to a distortion of the original unit. The play exists; the theoretical model does not. The function of Shakespeare's comedies is not to yield up a meta-form, Shakespearean comedy; the function of Shakespearean comedy, if it can persuasively be described, is to enable us better to understand any one comedy by Shakespeare. But one cannot accumulate data from certain plays, use them to construct a "genre" model that implies a more than cognate relationship with "genus," and then deploy the "genre" pattern as a triumphant interpretation of the difficulties of a recalcitrant specimen.[1] Hence I regard Shakespearean comedy as a theoretician's Grail, the pur-

---

[1] I have elaborated these objections in "Shakespearean Comedy and Northrop Frye," *Essays in Criticism* XXII (January, 1972).

suit of which may lead to a misjudgment of the individual comedy.

What, then, is a Shakespeare comedy? The category is established, for our purposes, by the Folio. No other authority or definition is available. The Folio classification is a loose, but convenient means of describing a play; and it doubtless represents broadly the expectations of Shakespeare's audience. "Comedy," for that audience, would signify a generally agreeable action and conclusion. It is a rough sort of contract between playwright and audience, modified by public awareness of Shakespeare's reputation but in no way committing the author to a formula. With this very broad license, Shakespeare, as I take it, initiates a number of widely different dramatic enterprises. Further than that I do not refine it, save in terms of the individual play. To expect more of "comedy" (with Shakespeare) is to court the danger which G. M. Young terms "one of the most insidious vices of the human mind: what the Germans in their terse and sparkling way call the hypostatization of methodological categories, or the habit of treating a mental convenience as if it were a real thing."[2] Can we agree to regard "a Shakespeare comedy" as a mental convenience, rather than a specimen of a definable genre, and take it on from there?

The formal limits of this study are the 10 comedies that run from *The Comedy of Errors* to *Twelfth Night*. I end with *Twelfth Night*, because I share the general critical agreement that that play concludes a phase in

[2] G. M. Young, *Victorian England* (London, 1960), p. 185.

Shakespeare's career. To continue with the problem comedies is to commit oneself to a coverage of the last plays, for I accord with those who see *All's Well That Ends Well* as an anticipation of the final romances. This study necessarily traces, in broad outline, Shakespeare's development in the comedies. That is however a consequence, rather than an aim, of the project. It is subordinate to the prime duty of interpreting each single comedy of Shakespeare's. Hence each chapter is devoted to a single play; and the object of each analysis is to detect the governing idea of the comedy, and to relate it to the action which expresses it. I seek to elicit the form of the comedy.

"Form," for our purposes, is organic form. This book is in no way concerned with abstract, or mechanical form. I look rather for patterns, for that element of repetition that guides us toward the play's principle of organization, and thus its design. No doubt one can say of a Shakespeare play, as a recent writer does of the sonnets, that it is "organized in a multitude of different coexistent and conflicting patterns."[3] I make no pretense of detecting all of the leading patterns in a play. But one can at least acknowledge a priority of patterns; and I attempt to describe the most significant of the patterns to impress themselves upon me. One has above all to grasp for the unity of the play, and that by the most direct route.[4]

[3] Stephen Booth, *An Essay on Shakespeare's Sonnets* (New Haven, 1969), p. ix.
[4] A most helpful definition of form, in the sense I adopt, is this: "In a broad sense, whatever in the make-up of an object helps one to perceive it as a whole is its form." V. M. Ames, in *A History of Philosophical Systems*, ed. V.T.A. Ferm (New

6

Schlegel's metaphor, the organism, is still I believe the best way of apprehending a Shakespeare play. But if one thinks of the critic as an expert in techniques, and thus committed to the mechanistic view of a play, then one has to concede that no single technique or set of techniques can be guaranteed to explain its workings. The interpreter of a Shakespeare play may approach it as a safe to be opened, his ear attuned to the click and fall of tumblers whose subtle alignments tell him that he is on the way to discovering its combination, until the door swings, as it seems, open. He will note now a piece of servant's gossip, parodying the pursuits of their social betters; now a cluster of images; now a marked repetition of certain literal, perhaps quite ordinary words; now a seeming irrelevance in the text, a clue not to be dismissed as a palimpsest of source revision; now a recurring situation, perhaps coded into a line in the first scene. Each sort of evidence has its function. An imagery approach, for instance, yields excellent results for *The Two Gentlemen of Verona*, yet is not I think helpful for *Much Ado About Nothing*. The comic-parody line explains much in *A Midsummer Night's Dream*, but fails to account for *The Merchant of Venice*. The concordances newly available cannot grasp the impalpabilities of human relationships, yet they may provide an intense illumination on a play's concerns via certain word-frequen-

---

York, 1950), p. 555. For Shakespearean form, the best account I know is in Hereward T. Price's *Construction in Shakespeare* (Ann Arbor, 1951), in which the key statement is: "His inner idea is manifested in an action, with which it is intimately fused." (p. 17)

cies. (The computer, it should be remembered, does its best work on quite ordinary words, such as "know" in *Much Ado About Nothing*, and "word" in *Love's Labour's Lost*.) Still, even this approach cannot be relied on to give immediate access to the heart of a play. The critic must borrow a portion of Shakespeare's infinite flexibility, in order to cope with him at all; and he must adapt his techniques to the particular challenge that each play presents.

I should like, then, to have each chapter judged as a separate enterprise, and not as the context for a recurring technique or critical preoccupation. Nor is each chapter a phase in a sustained argument on Shakespeare's development. Still, it would be useless to pretend that these separate interpretations do not, of themselves, present an argument of sorts. One inevitably arrives at a view of Shakespeare's techniques, concerns, and development, within the scope of this inquiry; and it seems best to record here the main conclusions to emerge.

The central technique of the comedies concerns the relation of the overtly comic parts to the rest of the play. Whenever one encounters a critic who writes of "comic relief" one can be fairly sure that he has misunderstood what is going on. The principle is that virtually all "comic" parts—and by that I mean passages centering on clowns, servants, jesters, and rustics—are extensions of the social function of a jester: they serve to criticize the behavior of their social superiors. This occurs in two ways: explicitly, through direct criticism, and implicitly, through parody. In the first category we can place, for

instance, Speed, Touchstone, and Feste, all of whom
have some interesting observations to make on the mores
of their betters. This type of clown, obviously, needs to
be a man of some intelligence. Subtler is the deployment
of the stupid clowns. In this category we can place Bottom, who enacts (with Titania, and his fellows) a burlesque of love, which is the main concern of the courtiers. But the best example of this category is Dogberry.
He provides, naturally, some good clean fun in the tradition that produces Mrs. Malaprop and rustic constabulary. Look at him and his myrmidons closely, though.
They are confronted with precisely the same situation
as their social betters; that is, they overhear things that
they were not meant to overhear. And, in their bumbling
way, they get it right. The detective techniques of Dogberry and Co. lead to the apprehension and conviction
of the criminals. Their betters fly to the wrong conclusions, fail to apply acceptable tests of hypotheses, and
are too busy, in Leonato's case, even to carry out their
duties as magistrate. Without the yokels, the gentry of
Messina would be lost. As Borachio sourly puts it:
"What your wisdoms could not discover, these shallow
fools have brought to light." The activities of the fools
in a Shakespearean comedy—whether or not they are
organized into a separate subplot—almost invariably
constitute a commentary on the main action. And that
commentary is often of a surprisingly tart flavor.

Much flows from this central technique. It helps to
grip, and confirm, the grand theme of the comedies,
which I take to be illusion. This theme can be thought
of as a broad band, running through nearly all the come-

dies. (It is not, I think, especially relevant to *The Merchant of Venice* in any but a very forced sense.) At one extreme of the band is simple error, the error of mistaken identity, as in *The Comedy of Errors* and *Twelfth Night*. This may be induced through disguise or likeness. Then comes deception, or error engineered, as in *Much Ado About Nothing*. At the other extreme are the follies of fantasy and self-deception, together with a rational failure to plumb fraud and deceptive appearances. Illusion in this sense ranges from the conventional, and role playing behavior of the young gentlemen of Verona, through the gyrations of the lovers in *A Midsummer Night's Dream*, to the fantasies of Orsino. The concept can be discussed in terms of psychology. It also emerges from certain passages of symbolic action, which dramatize in overt (even emblematic) or subtle form the idea of illusion. Thus, there are the masque/mask episodes in *Love's Labour's Lost* and *Much Ado About Nothing*; the "picture" (or "idol") passages in *The Two Gentlemen of Verona*; the application of the magic juice in *A Midsummer Night's Dream*; the messages of *Twelfth Night*. At such points the concerns of the play take on concrete, or manifest form. These symbolic proofs, which have, of course, their extension into the language of the plays, are to my mind the most convincing demonstration of illusion. It is for the most part the principals who are under the spell of illusion; that is why the commentary supplied by their social inferiors contributes so tellingly to the representation of the theme.

Opposed to illusion is, of necessity, reality. I use "reality" as an approximate way of describing the truth, or the inexorable facts of existence, that must challenge fantasy and error in all their forms, even in comedy. (Shakespeare never actually uses the word "reality." He sometimes employs "illusion": the resonance of "And here we wander in illusions" is especially striking. *The Comedy of Errors*, IV, 3, 38.) The presence of reality is crucial to an assessment of Shakespeare's comedies. "Tragedy is true guise; comedy lies" says Hardy; and the problem is to write comedies without telling lies. The problem is solved with astonishing mastery in *Love's Labour's Lost*, which I regard as the most open and explicit demonstration of Shakespeare's methods in the comedies. The young men make a frivolous and unrealistic vow; the women come, the courtly game is played out, and the young men are forsworn. But the festivities of the Court are stilled by the arrival of Mercade. The tidings he bears are of mortality: the King is dead. The party breaks up. There is no betrothal, but Berowne has to vow twelve months of what we should call social work, in a hospital. The play does not merely punish Berowne and his friends, it refutes them. Death, and the inexorable laws that are symbolized in oath-keeping, are the realities which the Shakespeare of *Love's Labour's Lost* warns us surely exist.

Now this is not a pattern that is crudely and overtly repeated in the other comedies. It is not necessary. One such demonstration, and of such severity, is enough. It is the extreme achievement of the vision that comprehends but does not deny the realities of life, even at the tableaux that precede the final curtain. "The words of Mercury are harsh after the songs of Apollo."

This, evidently, must make great demands on the dramatist's sense of tact and truth. The way out, as so often, is silence. Consider the conclusion of *The Two Gentlemen of Verona*, a title not without its ironies. Valentine rescues his betrothed, Silvia, from rape by his friend Proteus, and immediately hands her over to the would-be rapist, in token of magnanimity and eternal friendship. It is a gesture of sublime, fatuous egotism. One word from Silvia would explode Valentine's pretensions. But she says nothing. So Valentine is allowed to strut off stage in the full possession of his triumph. This is a fairly extreme instance of what is the normal Shakespearean method of handling realities in a comedy: to allow a sufficient exposure to certain views and facts that establish the situation, and then to elide or suppress them at the close so that the emotions generated by the final festivities will not be marred.

It will be evident by now that I am disinclined to stress the element of revelry in the comedies, and indeed I think that the term "festive comedy" can mask a misunderstanding of what is going on. To call the comedies "festive" is strictly accurate. Each of them ends in a feast, or dance, or wedding. So "festive" is a collective abstraction of plot. But the plot is only the most primitive of guides to our experience of a play. There is only the most general relationship between the festive experience—which is common to all men, and which is in part stimulated by the stage depiction of a feast—and our reception of the festivities in a Shakespeare comedy. That will depend upon the characteristics of the individual comedy. At each conclusion, one asks: how festive is this feast? How far have the problems of the comedy been resolved? I agree that the feast ending *The Comedy of Errors* does seem, absolutely and finally, to close the comedy. It is a call to revelry and reconciliation, and the critic need not hesitate to join the party. But from *The Taming of the Shrew* on, the feast embodies rather than terminates the conflicts of the play. That play ends on an open question ("'Tis a wonder, by your leave, she will be tamèd so"); and the same sort of doubt is more subtly expressed in the ambivalent, question begging conclusions of the later comedies. They trouble the audience afterwards. What manner of justice has been done to Shylock, or to Jessica? Why does the exiled Duke rush back to the meretricious delights of the Court, after crying up Arden in Act II? What sort of double marriage is it that is thrown together at the end of *Twelfth Night*? To speak of these conclusions as "clarifications" seems a considerable overstatement. If the endings were "clear," then critics ought to agree on their import. But they don't. I should prefer to see the conclusions of the middle comedies less as "clarifications" than as provisional re-groupings of situations that will continue their complex development.

I cannot, therefore, follow C. L. Barber in his contention that there is a sustained "correspondence between the whole festive occasion and the whole comedy."[5] Indeed, I cannot even identify the essence of a comedy which is called "festive," and distinguish it from a "non-

[5] C. L. Barber, *Shakespeare's Festive Comedy* (Princeton, 1959), p. 6.

festive" play. "Festivity" I regard as a part, but only a part, of the play. To make "the whole experience of the play like that of a revel"[6] is to simplify and thus to distort, through placing an exaggerated emphasis on what is in effect a synopsis of plot. To travel far along the "festive" road leads to this sort of judgment: "Craven or inadequate people appear, by virtue of the festive orientation, as would-be revellers, comically inadequate to hear the chimes at midnight. Pleasure thus becomes the touchstone for judgment of what bars it or is incapable of it."[7] And so the pleasure principle becomes the apex of a hierarchy of values. But the plays—and *Twelfth Night* is the test case—cannot support this. Even if "pleasure" is equated with Sir Toby's activities, and opposed to Malvolio's (but are not two different kinds of pleasure, or self-satisfactions involved?), the ending does not endorse Sir Toby's version, much less erect "pleasure" into an absolute. It merely points out the consequences that may follow from its indulgence. If one wants to derive a conclusion from Sir Toby's latter activities, it is simply that duelling when drunk is dangerous; especially if the other fellow happens to be sober. One can scarcely acclaim as the apotheosis of festivity a final dance from which the local lord of misrule is unavoidably absent, expiating in hospital his addiction to the pleasure principle.

In place of the pleasure principle, I advance the reality principle as the proper criterion of the conclusion, hence of the comedy as a whole. The great advantage of the reality principle is that it upholds no systems of values

[6] *Ibid.*, p. 6.   [7] *Ibid.*, p. 8.

whatsoever. It simply asserts that actions will have consequences. Some of them will be pleasant, and some not. Valentine, Orsino, Malvolio, and Falstaff are all governed by a species of fantasy; the last two are punished for it, the first two go their ways unchecked. This is an accurate indication of the personalities and social circumstances of the four. It does nothing to establish pleasure or any other value.

I suggest, therefore, that the comedies—from *The Merchant of Venice* on especially—organize our experience in a particular way: they permit a distance between our impulse to participate in the feast, and our awareness of the undercurrents and reservations present in the final situation. Or we might characterize the matter by distinguishing between the critic and member of the audience—one can be both, but (often) at different times. The playgoer is entitled to yield to the agreeable emotions of the final dance, especially if the production presents it as a communal accord. (The production may, of course, do otherwise. The leading theatrical practice of late years—I am thinking especially of the Royal Shakespeare Company—stresses the ironic and problematic aspects of the text. In this, theatrical practice is well ahead of academic criticism.) The critic, who may be the same playgoer, has a duty to reflect afterwards on certain nuances, on things that were said and left unsaid, done and left undone, that he did not fully take in during the performance. And he may then arrive at a different estimate of the action, and of the choices of interpretation that Shakespeare has built into the action. Generally, the critic who attends a Shakespearean revel

(I say nothing of the playgoer) would, I feel, be well advised to follow a simple precept: to stay sober. That way one appreciates more of the dance. No doubt Lepidus returned from Pompey's galley to assure his subordinates that Pompey had staged a superb affair, and that Antony and Octavius were really very friendly together. But the critic, confronted in imagination with the wine of Illyria, of Padua, and of Belmont, need not follow the example of the excellent Lepidus.

All this skirts around the question of laughter: and I ought to mention it here. There is something inherently absurd about the mass of commentary on Shakespeare's comedies, and the minute proportion of it concerned with the humor of the comedies, or even apparently aware that the plays are funny. Of course the critic can submit that he has no wish (or indeed competence) to reexamine the theories of Koestler, Bergson, Freud, et al.; or yet tediously expound a series of Shakespearean jokes. That is a reasonable line to take. Occasionally, though, a statement will surface that raises one's worst suspicions. A recent writer on the comedies, for example, unluckily volunteered this view (of the quartet of lovers in *A Midsummer Night's Dream*): "At no point in the play, unless it be the final scene, do we laugh either with or at them." For this display of insensibility, he was deservedly chidden by the reviewers; still, the matter has wide implications. We can set aside the possibilities that this particular critic preserves an excessive gravitas in the presence of a Shakespearean Comedy, or has been remarkably unfortunate in his productions of *A Midsummer Night's Dream*, and ask: how important to the reception of a comedy is laughter? Jonson thought "the moving of laughter is a fault in Comedie," and given the aims of his comedies—essentially, of social correction—one can see his point. No such extremity of doctrine applies to Shakespeare. It is impossible to draw up a lucid account of the matter, however, for at least two major reasons. First, the stimulus itself is a large variable. Productions, which are unique events, vary infinitely in their capacity and will to provoke laughter. And they make use of techniques ranging from the lowest buffoonery to the finest inflexion. Second, laughter itself is a purely physiological activity, that may be triggered by different sorts of stimuli and signify a range of feelings. Laughter may express hysteria, relief, surprise, hostility, anticipation, Hobbes' "sudden glory," and so on. It can be a complex affair. I suggest, for instance, that the scene in which Malvolio appears crossgartered is, curiously, a little less funny than the preceding letter scene. The audience is beginning to acquire a half-guilty awareness that the Joke is lumbering downhill, out of control. Guilt, delight, satisfied anticipation, the wish to punish the insufferable Malvolio, all figure in its reactions. Now these complex and variable affairs do not lend themselves to any sort of precise comment. Yet the comedies of Shakespeare yield, and are designed to yield, an infinity of laughter. Charles Gordon, surely the most urbane of writers on Shakespeare's comedies, was right in his advice to beware "les Tartuffes de la critique."[8]

[8] Charles Gordon, *Shakespearian Comedy and Other Studies* (Oxford, 1944), p. 6.

Still, one can acknowledge that laughter belongs to comedy, and yet see no great utility in investigating their relationship. I think it best to record the simple opinion that Shakespeare's comedies are extraordinarily funny; and that I have, personally, laughed inordinately at all of them in production. But the retailing of these agreeable experiences is not the concern of this book. There is a single exception to my avoidance of the topic. *The Merry Wives of Windsor* appears to me a machine for inducing laughter. Laughter is its end-product, not a by-product; its very form is a model for a theory of laughter. Hence I analyze the form of the play in terms of laughter mechanisms. For the rest, I think that the textual foundations for the audience's reactions can be studied as accurate accounts of human conduct, regardless of whether they give rise to laughter or not.[9]

This belief, or its opposite, is fundamental to any consistent view of the comedies. My assumption is that the behavior of the dramatis personae is, or ought to be, explicable in terms of naturalistic psychology. I take it to be axiomatic that Shakespeare's intuitive grasp of psychology is the foundation of his drama. Naturally, I am not prepared to defend to the death the credibility of (say) the 3rd Outlaw in *The Two Gentlemen of Verona*, or Dr. Caius in *The Merry Wives of Windsor*. Some allowance must be made for the exigences of playwriting.

[9] In this view, I am fortified by the anonymous writer of the Epistle prefacing the second Quarto of *Troilus and Cressida* (1609), who thought "this authors Commedies . . . so fram'd to the life, that they serve for the most common Commentaries of all the actions of our lives."

But to extend this license to the principal figures is, I hold, to misjudge Shakespeare's art. The alternative view, stated with admirable incisiveness by E. C. Pettet, is:

> A very large proportion of Shakespeare's young lovers, Valentine and Silvia, Lysander, Demetrius, Hermia and Helena, Bassanio (and much of Portia), Sebastian and Olivia, Claudio and Hero, along with their necessary friends, rivals, and parents, are simply pasteboard. They merely act out their tale of love-adventure. The tale is the thing, and Shakespeare never intended us to worry ourselves with their personalities and motives. In the main—though there are certain important exceptions—he was not much interested in the comedy of character.[10]

From this standpoint, Shakespeare (in the early comedies especially) is subordinating his gifts to the demands of the Romance tradition. These require a play that is essentially episodic, leaning heavily on exciting action and strong love interest. I, on the contrary, argue that even in the extreme case (*The Two Gentlemen of Verona*) the core of the play is a study in male psychology. Valentine is a portrait of conventional behavior, not a pasteboard brought into being by stage conventions. And even the wondrous events of the final scenes have a sort of hallucinatory conviction, as constituents of Valentine's mental landscape. As for the love interest in the romantic comedies, we should remember that "love" is

[10] E. C. Pettet, *Shakespeare and the Romance Tradition* (London, 1949), p. 86.

a broad term, comprising a wide variety of psychological conditions and actions. It is a word that people apply to their mental states, not a tight category that excludes psychological interest. The comedies, then, offer Shakespeare a recurring opportunity to anatomize "love." In short, I see Shakespeare as at all times able to build into it that apprehension of human personality (sketchily indicated at times, certainly) that controls his drama. He exploits the tradition; not it, him. The progress from the early to the later comedies is a story of technical diversification and growing complexity, not of a change in posture. The technical advance, from Speed to Rosalind/ Ganymede (representing the anti-Romantic voice) is enormous. But the same playwright remains, equally detached and equally determined to make his material serve his purpose.

What has changed is the scope of his enterprises. Broadly, they appear to be growing out all the time, to be accumulating more data within a single frame. A rough division is discernible between the early and later comedies among the plays we consider. The early comedies are more straightforward, single-minded exercises. One can say that *The Comedy of Errors* is a reconciliation, *The Two Gentlemen of Verona* a satiric demolition of gentlemanly poses, *Love's Labour's Lost* a refutation of folly, and *The Taming of the Shrew* a taming. From these four plays, one learns to recognize Shakespeare's handwriting in the comedies. After *A Midsummer Night's Dream*, something quite different seems to be happening. With *The Merchant of Venice*, fairly certainly 1596, a new kind of game makes its appearance. I can only characterize it very crudely, as the construction of two distinct plays within one frame. This is not the same as the levels-of-meaning view of Shakespearean drama, nor do I refer to the natural affinity of comedy and farce. *The Merchant of Venice* can be looked at as a species of melodrama—this is not an unsophisticated view, the most distinguished of critics hold it—or as an ironic comedy. *Much Ado About Nothing* can be regarded as a jolly elaboration of its title, or a serious analysis of modes of knowing (and naturally, a draft of *Othello*). *As You Like It* is an idyll, or a fairly perturbed pastoral. *Twelfth Night* is a warm-hearted defense of cakes and ale, or an inventory of illusions. In each case the comedy contains an exceptional range of tones, and of issues; and in each case the audience has some warrant, if it wishes, for classifying the comedy under Plays Pleasant or Plays Unpleasant. At the least, the alternative possibility is a factor in the audience's welcome of a Pleasant Comedy. The opposition between the bitter comedies of Jonson and the sweet comedies of Shakespeare is altogether too simple to be satisfying.

We need a term for the special type of play that Shakespeare is writing in this phase. I doubt if one exists, and that is merely to acknowledge openly that "type" is a false metaphor. One might call *The Merchant of Venice* a *drame*; but I can think of nothing that adequately describes *As You Like It* and *Twelfth Night*, or conveys their stereoscopic quality. Genre labels in this context pretend to objective description, but in fact supply interpretations. One is in the presence of a new phe-

21

nomenon. *As You Like It, or What You Will* seems the ideal device for these plays. They synthesize, as well as present, the main alternatives that I have suggested.

Still, the first of these alternatives merits only token discussion here. I judge it unnecessary to elaborate to my readers the romantic qualities of *The Merchant of Venice, Much Ado About Nothing, As You Like It*, and *Twelfth Night*. Nor shall I be concerned with the comedies' explicit treatment of love and its values. That is essentially an aspect of the plays' subject matter, and it has been admirably charted by John Russell Brown in *Shakespeare and His Comedies*. The emphasis in these studies is on the "other" play, the serious and at times somber presence that the comedies contain. These presences begin by mocking the figures in the foreground, and then turn imperceptibly to menacing them. The voice—it is the play's, not merely Speed's—that derides Valentine, then refutes Berowne, changes its tone during the interrogation of Antonio. Shylock has, for a moment, the task of examining the conventional wisdom of a public man; and his "directly interest" implies a vista on society that remains unexpunged by the events in Arden and Illyria. By the end of *Twelfth Night*, the presence that materializes in the destruction of Malvolio, and in Feste's rain, is seen to grimace at, if it does not openly threaten, the world of Orsino and Olivia. That presence is not identified with any one spokesman, yet Feste, like Touchstone, implies and seems aware of all that the play states. The nameless Fool who surfaces in *King Lear* to challenge authority, and identify itself, is no sudden apparition in Shakespeare's progress. He is the latest of

22

those clowns who have exposed the illusions of their masters; and he, like virtually all his fellows, constitutes a unit of intelligence that scrutinizes and ultimately challenges the world of their masters, "the great image of authority." One comes, then, to see the comedies as a means of preparation for the tragedies. That is the effect, if not the purpose, of the dramas that I discern. The tragedies were always present in the comedies; and they were always going to be written. The conclusions implied, but not stated in the comedies, were one day to be pursued.

CHAPTER I

"And here we wander in illusions"

Few people come to *The Comedy of Errors* save via
many other plays in the canon. One tends to see it less as
a play in its own right than as an anticipation of what
Shakespeare is to write. It is the first and last time in
which he bases a play on the simple central principle of
mistaken identity. The conclusion is obvious: we have
here what is essentially an exercise in the dramatist's
craft, a well-judged decision to master the mechanical
elements of a comedy before proceeding to the more exacting challenges. Hence the widely held critical view
that this is the first of Shakespeare's comedies: he would
neither have wanted nor needed to have written it after
his first essay. One looks then for the seeds that will ger-
minate later. And naturally, one finds them. But given
this disposition to the play one can merit Dr. Johnson's
epitome of Upton, that he did not readily miss what he
sought to find. As I shall later suggest, *The Comedy of
Errors* has in an important respect been improperly inter-
preted in the light of the later comedies. Much of what
emerges from *The Comedy of Errors* must apply, naturally and unforcedly, to the subsequent comedies. This is
plain if we consider the genre, theme, and form of the
play.

24

I

The Comedy of Errors is a comedy by title and by classification in the Folio, that repository of coarse distinctions. We normally refine on this by terming the play a farce. It is in fact two plays, a farce and a comedy, most expertly synthesized. Farce, essentially mechanistic, requires that we look on all of the dramatis personae from outside. It is an assumption of the genre that they are merely simulacra of human beings, for that part of our minds which, in drama, assents to the proposition that they are real people with real problems is tranquilized or inhibited. But Shakespeare presents characters from the inside, that is to say he depicts people who have stumbled into the world of farce and do not understand its laws. The farce play here is merely the record of the mechanical errors based on mistaken identity. The comedy is the study of the reactions of the characters to the farce in which they find themselves. (One could call the play "Six characters in search of themselves—and a genre.") There are, then, two major objections to terming *The Comedy of Errors* a farce; the frame to the action, pregnant with tragedy, and the fact that the characters consistently refuse to be mechanized.

The subject matter of the play, evidently, is error. But this is of no interest here whatsoever. The situation is static.[1] We are fully apprised of it from the start and it is capable only of complication, not of development. The theme that emerges is the quest for identity,[2] and

---

[1] Bertrand Evans, *Shakespeare's Comedies* (Oxford, 1960), p. 2.
[2] In these terms the play has been discussed by R. A. Foakes

this concerns only the underlying play of *The Comedy of Errors*. And this theme requires us at once to examine the form of the comedy. As is customary in Shakespeare, the form is the manifestation of a structural idea which is simple and profound, though not so simply articulated in critical terms. The structural idea of *The Comedy of Errors* I apprehend to be the union of two halves, each seeking the other, paralleling and complementing the other, ultimately to be reconciled.

II

The locale embodies this concept of form. The later Shakespearean device, as we know, is to relate behavior to two local nuclei of contrasted values; say, the cold intellect of Venice to the emotion and unreason of Othello's Cyprus. Here, the action takes place entirely in Ephesus; but it is constantly matched with Syracuse; and Syracuse is seen as in all essential respects identical with Ephesus. They produce the same sort of person, and they parallel each other's laws; the Duke, indeed, insists on applying the death penalty to Egeon precisely because the Syracusans have persecuted the Ephesan merchants. (I, 1, 5-10) (To that extent the Law of the opening scene is far from "irrational";[3] the Duke, in all statecraft, can do little else but enforce a *tu quoque*.) The Duke's opening speech reveals a legal separation,

---

in his New Arden edition of *The Comedy of Errors* (London, 1962), pp. xliii-xlix.

[3] Northrop Frye, *A Natural Perspective: The Development of Shakespearean Comedy and Romance* (New York, 1965), p. 73.

26

a total distinction of identity between Syracuse and Ephesus. Yet this distinction is a pure legality; in human terms there is none, for humanity spans Ephesus and Syracuse on equal terms. The matter becomes especially interesting, psychologically, at the points where Antipholus of Syracuse reacts to the apparently eccentric behavior of the Ephesan natives.

> They say this town is full of cozenage:
> As, nimble jugglers that deceive the eye,
> Dark-working sorcerers that change the mind,
> Soul-killing witches that deform the body,
> Disguisèd cheaters, prating mountebanks,
> And many such-like liberties of sin:
>
> (I, 2, 97-102)

And see also III, 2, 154-155; IV, 3, 10-11. Here Antipholus, in a revealing spasm of instant paranoia, transforms the near-identical "other" to an alien stereotype. But the representatives of each city seek, blunder toward, and ultimately find their siblings and mates. The oceanic message of this play, perhaps the sole truly festive of the comedies, is that the worlds of Ephesus and Syracuse are at one.

That is the organic principle. The personal relations—there are four sets, who mount multiple crossrelationships—all exhibit "other"-seeking, or centripetal tendencies. Egeon sets this pattern. He seeks, for his son's sake, his lost wife and son. (I, 1, 124-139) There is a sense of tragic *incompleteness* about him, aside from the impending execution: "Hopeless to find, yet loath to leave unsought" (I, 1, 135), and "Hopeless and helpless doth

27

Egeon wend,/But to procrastinate his lifeless end." (I, 1, 157-158) His final union with Emilia and his sons reverses a personal tragedy, completes an incomplete man, and crowns the festivity of recognitions.

The Antipholi set up a subtler set of relations with each other, and with their womenfolk. Antipholus of Syracuse is the more interesting of the two. A melancholy fellow, embryo to Hamlet, he seems a spiritual younger brother in search of an elder. He has nothing like that certitude of identity that his brother has. Antipholus of Syracuse values Dromio for amusing him "When I am dull with care and melancholy" (I, 2, 20); then, significantly, "I will go lose myself" (I, 2, 30) preludes an aimless wandering into town. His state of mind finds expression in this:

> He that commends me to mine own content,
> Commends me to the thing I cannot get.
> I to the world am like a drop of water
> That in the ocean seeks another drop,
> Who falling there to find his fellow forth,
> Unseen, inquisitive, confounds himself.
> So I, to find a mother and a brother,
> In quest of them, unhappy, lose myself.
>
> (I, 2, 33-40)

The "drop of water" image is at the core of this play. Repeated in a later scene (II, 2, 124-128) it links with the sea—a literal background which, as I have suggested, has its significance here—and conveys the deep sense of incompleteness that weighs on the characters of

28

The Comedy of Errors. And this, one notes, antedates and is independent of the errors of the action. Shakespeare is evidently intent on writing a play that is quite separate from the mechanical provision of laughs through confusion of identity.

The problem of identity is connected with that of names. (A Shakespearean preoccupation that is to find its culmination in the situation of Coriolanus, "a kind of nothing, titleless," without the new name of "Romanus.") Antipholus of Syracuse takes names as a proof of identity: "How can she thus then call us by our names?/ Unless it be by inspiration." (II, 2, 165-166) It is a test of reality, an echo of Egeon's statement that the twins "could not be distinguished but by names." (I, 1, 52) Antipholus needs these assurances, for his sense of identity—never very strong—is rapidly weakened by the assured behavior of the Ephesans:

> To me she speaks; she moves me for her theme.
> What, was I married to her in my dream?
> Or sleep I now, and think I hear all this?
> What error drives our eyes and ears amiss?
> (II, 2, 180-183)

He yields readily to the notion that he is in a dream, that *his* identity is lost: "I think thou art [transformed], and so am I." (II, 2, 195) The doubt is echoed in "If everyone knows us, and we know none,/'Tis time, I think, to trudge, pack, and be gone." (III, 2, 150-151) And so to the *cri de coeur* that seems to linger long after his reintegration with the community: "The fellow is distract,

29

and so am I;/And here we wander in illusions." (IV, 3, 37-38) The pregnant "illusions" refers to an area of drama to which "error" is merely the signpost. For Antipholus of Syracuse, identity is to be confirmed by something other than a correction of error. We do not know what he makes of his long-sought brother at the end, for he does not tell us; by then it is clear that his most important relationship is with Luciana, his sexual complement. It is Luciana that satisfies his drive toward identity: "It is thyself, mine own self's better part;/Mine eye's clear eye, my dear heart's dearer heart." (III, 2, 61-62) He needs a brother and a wife; with them, and parents restored, his quest for identity is at an end.[4]

His brother, Antipholus of Ephesus suffers a totally different loss of identity. As R. A. Foakes remarks, he, "by contrast, regards himself as alone sane in a world gone mad."[5] In the play's design he is the temperamental complement of his brother; his explanation of a disordered world is that the others are mad or leagued in conspiracy against him. The proud, self-sufficient man of property, bound in a dark room, is a note whose significance in Shakespeare's future no one fails to recognize, but it is allowed to develop no overtones here. The interest attaches rather to Antipholus's standing as a merchant, and his relations with his wife. And here, too, we move to a character who feels herself to be incomplete.

---

[4] The identity theme is discussed at further length by A. C. Hamilton, *The Early Shakespeare* (San Marino, California, 1967), pp. 90-108.

[5] Foakes, *op.cit.*, p. xlvii.

Adriana is discovered lacking her husband's presence, "Neither my husband nor the slave returned," as she tells us in her opening breath. (II, 1, 1) His absence from dinner symbolizes the problems of their marriage, and her concern. The relationship between Adriana and Antipholus of Ephesus, nominally a union, is in fact flawed; the two halves seek from the other what they do not find.

This is a relationship that we have, I think, to get right in order to appreciate the design of the play. I cannot follow the idea that the play is a tract on the evils of possessiveness in love: "it deals . . . not with the joys of giving in love, but with the follies and evils of love. Adriana's idea of love is to try to maintain a hold over her husband; the liberty of his actions galls her and she demands her rights."[6] Adriana's view of love is scarcely central to the play, however one assesses it; and to denounce the "possessiveness" of Adriana seriously overstates the situation. In these matters Shakespeare is careful to give everyone a case, and while Adriana is doubtless in the Roman tradition of the the the shrew,[7] the contours are much softened. She is presented as an intelligent and independent woman fretting against an un-

[6] John Russell Brown, *Shakespeare and His Comedies* (London, 1957), p. 54. This view is broadly supported by Peter G. Phialas, *Shakespeare's Romantic Comedies: The Development of their Form and Meaning* (Chapel Hill, North Carolina, 1966), p. 12; and Harold Brooks, "Themes and Structure in *The Comedy of Errors*," in *Early Shakespeare*, ed. John Russell Brown and Bernard Harris (London, 1961), p. 66.

[7] H. B. Charlton, *Shakespearian Comedy* (London, 1938), pp. 68-70.

31

reasonable social framework rather than one unreasonable in herself. Her scene with Luciana (II, 1) appears to place her within the Euripides-Shaw tradition of females who are in no way inclined to defer to the mores of a masculine society: "Why should their liberty than ours be more?" (II, 1, 10) is the position she defends against the passive Luciana, all for deferring to the dominant male. The course of the play, however, suggests that this is essentially an argument that Adriana is making use of to justify her disquiet. She is, quite simply, terrified of losing her husband; to regain him, and not a proto-Fabian liberty of action, is her desire. The "vine" image that she deploys (II, 2, 173-179) reflects more accurately her concept of the marital state. And

> Ah, but I think him better than I say,
> And yet would herein others' eyes were worse.
> Far from her nest the lapwing cries away;
> My heart prays for him, though my tongue do curse.
>
> (IV, 2, 25-28)

reveals the truth of her anguish and her fears. Certainly she has overdone her complaints, as her implicit admission at the end, in the face of Emilia's rebuke, makes clear. "He did betray me to mine own reproof." (V, 1, 90) But this is not at all the same thing as saying that she has no grounds for complaint. After all, Antipholus of Ephesus himself sketches in a justification for Adriana:

> I know a wench of excellent discourse,
> Pretty and witty, wild and yet, too, gentle.
> There will we dine. This woman that I mean,

My wife—but I protest, without desert—
Hath oftentimes upbraided me withal:

(III, 1, 109-113)

Men who make a habit of visiting a courtesan, purely
for the good food and high quality of conversation, must
expect to have these blameless motives misinterpreted.
The audience is put in the position of a divorce court
judge, who unsurprisingly concludes on the evidence that
both sides have a case. No *prima causa* of the marital
discord is indicated; it is a technique that Shakespeare
preserves intact in his study of Iago-Emilia, the heart of
Othello. It is, I suggest, essential to maintain a critical
objectivity in this marital imbroglio and do as Shakespeare does—avoid taking sides.

There remains the Dromios. They have, in the main,
the function of comically extending the qualities of their
masters. The Syracusan Dromio, like his master, sees
strange shapes in the exotic behavior of the Ephesans.
But while Antipholus had seen "soul-killing witches" (I,
2, 100) and "Lapland sorcerers" (IV, 3, 11), his servant
perceives "goblins, elves, and sprites." (II, 2, 189) These
homelier and less fearsome creatures compose a nicely
graduated modulation of his master's voice. And the
Syracusan Dromio's wooing by Nell (III, 2) is of course
a gross parody of Adriana's approaches to her supposed
husband. Here, again, is a technique of bedrock significance in the development of Shakespeare's comedies. It
is a safe generalization that Shakespeare's clowns are
never merely funny; they always provide some form of
commentary on or parody of their social betters. Now

the Ephesan Dromio is used to underline the psychological facts of his master's experience. This, his key speech, can safely be played on the stage to extract all possible laughs:

> I am an ass indeed; you may prove it by my long ears. I have served him from the hour of my nativity to this instant, and have nothing at his hands for my service but blows. When I am cold, he heats me with beating. I am waked with it when I sleep, raised with it when I sit, driven out of doors with it when I go from home, welcomed home with it when I return; nay, I bear it on my shoulders as a beggar wont her brat; and I think when he hath lamed me, I shall beg with it from door to door.
>
> (IV, 4, 27-36)

But the lament parallels the bewilderment of Antipholus of Ephesus at a world which has suddenly turned vicious on him. It is the sharply caught apprehension of what it must be like to be a servant in a world of mad masters, to be sane and yet in an impotent minority.

To these extensions of their superiors falls the final ritual of reconciliation. Father and mother, brother and brother, husband and wife, lover and betrothed, all come together at the close. "The gossips' or baptismal feast affirms relationship and identity";[8] the halves come together. Syracuse comes to Ephesus, and the baggage, it seems, is to be transferred from the waiting ship after all. (v, 1, 410-414) "Embrace thy brother there, rejoice with him" the Syracusan Antipholus enjoins his servant:

[8] Brooks, op.cit., p. 68.

and the Dromios, the humblest of the dramatis personae, stay to enact the union of which the origin, and symbol, is the ovum. "We came into the world like brother and brother;/And now let's go hand in hand, not one before another." (v, 1, 427-428)

III

The mechanism by which two sets of actors relate to each other is the exchange of money and the chain. These concrete objects become the foci of crosspurposes.[9] It is not necessary to follow the details of the misunderstandings, but it is important to assess the central significance of the device. The physical/verbal emphasis is consistent: "chain" occurs 45 times, and "gold" (with compounds) 32 times. They compose an early test case of Shakespearean symbolism. The issue is very simple. What does "gold," with "chain," signify?

The first law of Shakespearean symbolism is that it is never forced. The symbolic implications flow easily and naturally from the literal object (or activity), which itself appears to emerge inevitably from the course of the play. This quality of naturalness is, moreover, perfectly compatible with the formal or even emblematic poses into which the characters on occasion seem to stiffen. In *The Comedy of Errors* the use made of "gold" (and "money," and "chain") compels two questions: what are the natural associations of "gold," and what associations are especially generated in the context of the play?

The second question dominates the first, for "gold,"

[9] *Ibid.*, p. 57.

clearly, has tremendous positive and negative potentialities. In Jonson, Middleton, and Tourneur, for example, "gold" can symbolize the moral corruption of a society in which human values are reduced to economic terms. But equally, "gold" can signify an easeful, harmonious fertility, a symbol of man's wealth that parallels nature's abundance. So there is no obvious restriction to the natural values of "gold." If, however, we examine its employment in *The Comedy of Errors*, it is plainly regarded as an instrument of communication. It is this, and not exploitation or possessiveness, that extends the meaning of "gold."

It is, perhaps, useful to record certain unexceptionable banalities here, for they help to clarify one's conception of Shakespeare's mind in action. Money, then, is necessary to a society, because it is a fundamental mechanism for communication and for ordering relationships. Hence money (or gold, or cowrie-shells) has in itself no moral values whatsoever; it serves merely to identify the moral values of whichever person is using it. Possessive people manipulate gold possessively, generous people give it away freely. One has to avoid a stock response to "gold" (and also, "chain") as something with innate criminal tendencies. Now in this play, no one *uses* gold as a means of expressing personality, or of controlling others. It is purely a mode of doing business, and (for Adriana) of confirming that a promise will be kept. That, indeed, is the substance of its meaning for her. The recent critical tendency to allow the obvious implications of "chain" to wander into the field, designated as Adriana's "possessiveness" has little foundation in the text. For Adriana's attitude is stated in her first reference to it: "Sister, you know he promised me a chain" (II, 1, 106); and the word *promise*, with its associates of bond-holding and oath-keeping is the major underlying concept. If Adriana had harped on "chain" more than the others, one could allow a certain associative transference, but in fact she does not. I see no ironic juxtaposition of personal and commercial values in this play.

The trouble, I think, lies in the magnetic pull of *The Merchant of Venice*. That play analyzes human and commercial values in detached and potentially critical fashion: "gold" in that comedy is different from "gold" in *The Comedy of Errors*. One can rarely make constant equations when talking of a Shakespearean symbol. If it is necessary to use another play to interpret *The Comedy of Errors*, then we can turn to *Love's Labour's Lost*. That play is based on oath-keeping, and advances a total refutation of a frivolous failure to keep one's word. It is the word-oath idea, and not the less pleasant aspects of money, that are awakened by the merchants' altercation of IV, 1 in *The Comedy of Errors*. There is no question of the merchants behaving irrationally or unreasonably in this demand for payment. These people are no Shylocks. Their talk of "discharging bonds" is the legitimate business of a just society, and there is no hint of irony in Angelo's tribute to Antipholus as one of "credit infinite, highly beloved." (v, 1, 6)

In sum, "gold" and "chain" are deployed objectively and neutrally here. The resonances latent in "gold" are stilled; the musician places his hand on the string. All that is important is to note what gold is used for: to

37

communicate, to fix a promise and to identify its redemption. Gold (as for the clowns-realists in *Love's Labour's Lost*) is the measure and the test of reality. "You saw they speak us fair; give us gold" (IV, 4, 150) says the Syracusan Dromio, applying this simple test to bizarre events; and at the end his master assents to the same demonstration:

Syr. Ant.: If this be not a dream I see and hear.
Angelo: That is the chain, sir, which you had of me.
Syr. Ant.: I think it be, sir; I deny it not.

(V, 1, 378-380)

The writing of *The Comedy of Errors* is distinguished by a rigid concentration on the work in hand. It contains at least two major seams that ask to be mined: the ideas of gold-credit-value, and the situation of law infringed. But the iron demands of a comedy solely based on mistaken identity mean that these temptations (as surely they must have been) are suppressed. Those rich seams would have been incompatible with the development of this play. An ironic analysis of mercantile values destroys the simple fun of honest businessmen confounded in the pursuance of their calling; the law infringed can only gather weight if Egeon has, in some way, merited his official fate. But the law, though reasonable in context, has no real connection at all with any human misdeed committed by Egeon. The only theme that can emerge naturally from the situation of mistaken identity, is precisely that of identity; the dramatic disquisitions are consequent upon the text selected.

"Error" is illusion mechanized, and *The Comedy of*

Errors is the first in the sequence of comedies that examine the implications of error: the chain stretches ahead to *A Midsummer Night's Dream, Much Ado About Nothing,* and *Twelfth Night.* It is the first, too, to set the pattern of fractured communication that is the skeleton of *Twelfth Night.* And the situation of Dr. Pinch and the merchant of Ephesus contains the first faint tremors of the storm that is to blow up over the heath. Camus' image is appropriate: nothing is more interesting in *The Comedy of Errors* than to see the dark wind from the horizon of Shakespeare's future, blowing toward him.

CHAPTER II

Love and Freindship

No exercise of critical muscularity can make of *The Two Gentlemen of Verona* a neglected masterpiece. But this play still needs to be saved from its critics, most of whom, strong in the sense of numbers, have joined hands to dance around the remains of that curiosity, a bad Shakespearean play. For my part, I think that the qualities that are effortlessly recognized in the Shakespearean canon as a whole should induce a certain caution, before we yield to the impulse to write this play off as a rather badly judged experiment by the early Shakespeare. The early Shakespeare, after all, is only our shorthand for the earliest Shakespeare that we know. He was probably nearly thirty when he wrote *Two Gentlemen*; not exactly a novice at life, or anything else. Is it not possible that in dismissing this piece as a tedious concession to contemporary conventions, we may have got it wrong?

Most of the critics of this play have, I believe, misjudged its drift.[1] Here is one view that serves as a start-

[1] Critics—there are not many—who stress the satiric elements in *The Two Gentlemen of Verona*, include Ulrici, and in the twentieth century Hereward T. Price, "Shakespeare as a Critic," *Philological Quarterly*, xx (1941), 390-399: and Clifford Leech, in his introduction to the New Arden edition of *The Two Gentlemen of Verona* (London, 1969).

ing point. I quote it because it embodies classically what I hold to be the wrong view of *Two Gentlemen*:

> Shakespeare was unable to maintain in his dramatic treatment the necessary balance between the Romance convention within which he was working and the kind of characterization demanded by this convention. Valentine is obviously intended to be the focus of romantic sympathy as an attractive, idealistic young man. . . .
>
> Perhaps the best illustration, however, of the playwright being led by his dramatic instincts and his interest in human nature, to overload his conventional framework occurs in the final scene. . . .
>
> . . . for brief moments during the play he has managed to lift some of his creations out of the original Romance framework he adopted; and at this point his success in having done so will not allow them to be fitted back again into the two-dimensional mold.[2]

That is to say, the twin poles of the Romantic conventions and natural characterization create opposed demands that destroy the play. This is basically a revision of Charlton's verdict: "Clearly, Shakespeare's first attempt to make romantic comedy had only succeeded so far that it had unexpectedly and inadvertently made romance comic."[3]

And this, with its astonishing adverbs, "unexpectedly,"

[2] Norman Sanders, ed., *The Two Gentlemen of Verona*, New Penguin edn. (Harmondsworth, England, 1968), pp. 13, 39.

[3] H. B. Charlton, *Shakespearian Comedy* (London, 1938), p. 43.

41

"inadvertently," stems in turn from the seventeenth century, and the idea of Shakespeare as a gifted natural, a master of serendipity. Charlton's epitome focuses the issue with great precision. But the play, to be understood, requires a reversal of the majority vote.

The Two Gentlemen of Verona is an experiment, but a controlled experiment. Shakespeare does not "inadvertently" stumble into his design, which is to make comedy out of romance. That design is plain from the opening speech of the play; it does not merely evolve later. The notion emerges, from the critical consensus, of the Romantic conventions controlling Shakespeare. On the contrary, *Two Gentlemen* reveals Shakespeare depicting people as deeply under the spell of conventions. Conventions, in other words, are not simply a code of writing plays, but of behavior in life. To understand *Two Gentlemen* it is necessary to see Valentine and Proteus as two role-playing young men (Valentine especially) who adhere to a fantastic code of conventional behavior. Thus the climax of the final scene in no way impairs the psychological credibility of the action. It is merely Shakespeare's mode of synthesizing the requirements of the conventions, and of life. In the climax of *Two Gentlemen* can be seen one of the earliest examples of the inexorable organic logic of a Shakespeare play, achieving a conclusion that is astonishing, but inevitable. It is like the coup of a chess master whose final combination crowns the approach-work of many moves. And nowadays one awards the *prix de beauté* not to the startling conclusion, but to the preparation that has made it logical.

I

To our analysis of the play, then. As is usual in a Shakespeare play, the opening lines merit the closest attention:

Valentine: Cease to persuade, my loving Proteus;
Home-keeping youth have ever homely wits.
Were't not affection chains thy tender days
To the sweet glances of thy honored love,
I rather would entreat thy company
To see the wonders of the world abroad
Than, living dully sluggardis'd at home,
Wear out thy youth with shapeless idleness.
But since thou lov'st, love still, and thrive
    therein,
Even as I would when I to love begin.

                                      (I, 1, 1-10)

Valentine is praising conventional behavior. It is proper for young men to travel, hence he intends to travel. The generalization of line 2 is an index to his mind; the general conditions his specific behavior. The point, though, lies in the tail of his speech. Proteus is a lover, hence a quite different set of values applies to him; and Valentine quite approves of this, too. Hence the give-away final line, "Even as I would, when I to love begin." That line affords the essence of Valentine. It recognizes that when the times comes for Valentine to play the role of lover, he will do so with an entire acceptance of its requirements. Behavior is governed by convention.

43

Hence Valentine, friend but not (as yet) lover, does the conventional thing in mocking the situation of his friend. His raillery of Proteus (i, 1, 29-35) reveals him entering wholeheartedly into the spirit of the role. And the essential immaturity of both young men is well implied in the repeated "writers say." (i, 1, 42, 45) Each needs an authority of sorts to govern his behavior. It is worth adding that in this play as in *Love's Labour's Lost* the opening contains an unrealistic vow. The effect of this comparison is to suggest that Shakespeare looks upon the whole transaction much more skeptically than is at first apparent, for in *Love's Labour's Lost* the matter is very much sharpened. The young men of *Two Gentlemen*, as in *Love's Labour's Lost*, are early seen to be fixed in a strong vein of attitudinizing.

This becomes fully apparent in ii, 1, as Valentine enters upon his next role, that of lover. (A role, significantly, that he has "learned," as Speed sardonically notes. ii, 1, 18) His language, figuring the whole play, is a send-up of the Romantic conventions: "Sweet ornament, that decks a thing divine!" he gasps, over Silvia's glove. (ii, 1, 5) In this, Valentine is being perfectly consistent with himself—the conventions require one to ring the changes of behavior as the role changes; but it is nonetheless true, as Speed points out, that the changes involved are ridiculous. A key image motif is initiated to make this point. Valentine is "metamorphosed with a mistress," according to Speed (ii, 1, 28-29); the word repeats Proteus' "Thou, Julia, thou hast metamorphosed me." (i, 1, 66) Moreover, the idea extends to "chameleon," for the "chameleon Love" jest of Speed (II, 1, 158) alludes to that animal's capacity for instant change of color—according to its situation—as well as its feeding on air. "Chameleon," in fact, is a witty symbol for the young lovers, and Thurio too has to endure its application. (II, 4, 25)

Speed develops his critical appreciation of his master's folly in the remarkable "figure" passage that follows Valentine's presentation of the letter to Silvia. It is an early instance of Shakespeare presenting the symbolic through a literal passage rich in significance. For, as Speed points out, "O excellent device—was there ever heard a better?/That my master being scribe, to himself should write the letter!" (II, 1, 129-130) That is it, exactly; for the letter, nominally directed at Silvia's "friend," really, to Silvia, is most aptly redirected to Valentine. For it is, in a sense, written to himself, to his personal idol, not a real woman, Silvia. The letter is a noncommunication, a monument to his role playing, that precisely foreshadows the play's climax in which Silvia ceases altogether to *be*. Self-absorption, at all times, is the clue to Valentine's conduct.

The inherent anomalies in the relations between the two egotists of Verona become apparent in II, 4. The roles are reversed from the opening scene; Proteus is now the skeptical friend, Valentine the despairful lover, whose description of his pangs leaves little to the imagination: "Ay, Proteus, but that life is altered now," and so on through a catalogue of woes. (II, 4, 125-139) To which Proteus, gazing on the miniature of Silvia, affixes

45

the right term: "Was this the idol that you worship so?"
(II, 4, 141) The "idol" image is the central one here-
abouts. It is extended into Proteus'

> For now my love is thawed,
> Which, like a waxen image 'gainst a fire
> Bears no impression of the thing it was.
>
> (II, 4, 197-199)

The metaphor is strengthened by the Duke's repetition
of it later:

> This weak impress of love is as a figure
> Trenchèd in ice, which with an hour's heat
> Dissolves to water and doth lose his form.
>
> (III, 2, 6-8)

As, in these two instances, the love/image/figure-analogy
is associated with change, it links with the "chameleon"
idea. And the visual implications of "idol" are elaborated into Proteus' " 'Tis but her picture I have yet
beheld,/And that hath dazzlèd my reason's light." (II,
4, 206-207) A nice inversion, this; Valentine makes an
"idol" out of a reality, a living woman; Proteus a reality
out of an "idol," a picture. It is another passage of trans-
parent symbolism. "Idol" is the satiric reduction of
Antipholus of Syracuse's "mine own self's better part."
In brief, the image-cluster that comprises "chameleon,"
"idol," "image," "figure" is the central one of the play.
It projects the ideas of illusion and change that are associated with love, and is later to be absorbed in the implications of "shadow" and "picture." These latter terms

refer to a concrete object, hence the course of the play effortlessly dramatizes ideas originally introduced as metaphors.

The ironies of ii, 4, then, contain the key to this comedy. They are pleasantly enough handled by Shakespeare; particularly disarming is Valentine's departure to keep an eye on Thurio, coupled with his explanation: ". . . and I must after,/For love, thou know'st, is full of jealousy." (ii, 4, 173-174) The "thou know'st" is especially revealing; Valentine, half-apologetically, is explaining that he *has* to do this, it is the done thing for lovers. The ironies are plain enough in iii, 1, when Valentine, left to himself, laments the failure of his plans for elopement. He observes, quite truthfully—in a sense he cannot comprehend—

To die is to be banished from myself.
And Silvia is myself; banished from her
Is self from self.

(iii, 1, 171-173)

And, in a line of finality, "She is my essence." (iii, 1, 182) True: she has no external life from himself. Silvia as a stage being may lead an autonomous life, but in Valentine's mind she has largely the status of anima. Hence there is a frosty irony underlying the song title for which the play is best known. Who, indeed, *is* Silvia? And what is she?

For Proteus, as for Valentine, she is essentially another variety of idol. The point is again hammered in, through the dialogue of iv, 2 that repeats the motif:

47

Proteus: Madame, if your heart be so obdurate,
          Vouchsafe me yet your picture for my love,
          The picture that is hanging in your chamber:
          To that I'll speak, to that I'll sigh and weep;
          For, since the substance of your perfect self
          Is else devoted, I am but a shadow,
          And to your shadow will I make true love.
Julia: [Aside] If 'twere a substance, you would, sure,
              deceive it
          And make it but a shadow, as I am.
Silvia: I am very loath to be your idol, sir.
          But, since your falsehood shall become you
              well
          To worship shadows and adore false shapes . . .
                                    (IV, 2, 119-130)

It is an analysis of the situation that covers Valentine just as much as Proteus. And the scene that extends the promise (IV, 4) clinches the matter. Julia's reactions to the painting of Silvia are interesting. (IV, 4, 182-199) She sees clearly that the differences between her looks, and Silvia's, do not account for the "idolatry." (198) Julia's meditation foreshadows the idea of the interchangeability of the love object, that plays so large a part in *A Midsummer Night's Dream* and *Twelfth Night*. And her conclusion

What should it be that he respects in her
But I can make respective in myself
If this fond Love were not a blinded god?
Come, shadow, come and take this shadow up,
For 'tis thy rival. O thou senseless form,

Thou shalt be worshipped, kissed, loved, and adored!
And, were there sense in his idolatry,
My substance should be statue in thy stead.

(IV, 4, 192-199)

rounds off the image motif that dominates the play for—
typically for a heroine in the comedies—love involves
no illusion whatsoever. She sees very clearly the self-
delusion and inconstancy of the male, yet takes Proteus
for what he is. The contrast between the male and female
roles is exact, and merciless.

II

The climax to the action is the reductio ad absurdum
of the role playing that has characterized the conduct
of the male lead. Valentine, intervening in the intended
rape, disposes of Silvia to the rapist upon a vow of re-
pentance. It is pure drama of sensibility. The twenty-
four lines of the Valentine-Proteus exchange compose as
Miss Bradbrook remarks, "the germ or core of the
play."[4] With the essential sense of this I agree, but I think
the metaphor may be misleading. The "germ" of a Shakespeare play is found, organically, in the opening passages; the conclusion is the inexorable manifestation of
growth tendencies that have driven the action of the play.
Shakespeare does not contrive a conclusion; he reveals
that a given outcome must necessarily be so. And it is so
here. The magnanimous/fatuous/ungentlemanly action
of Valentine in disposing of Silvia, a stage prop in the

[4] M. C. Bradbrook, *Shakespeare and Elizabethan Comedy*
(London, 1951), p. 151.

drama of Valentine, has excited the horror of critics on moral or aesthetic grounds. But this act, theatrical and compelling as it is, is merely the consequence and embodiment of the speech that precedes it.

Valentine: Thou common friend, that's without faith or love,
For such is a friend now. Treacherous man,
Thou hast beguiled my hopes. Naught but mine eye
Could have persuaded me. Now I dare not say
I have one friend alive; thou wouldst disprove me.
Who should be trusted, when one's right hand
Is perjurèd to the bosom? Proteus,
I am sorry I must never trust thee more,
But count the world a stranger for thy sake.
The private wound is deepest. O time most accurst,
'Mongst all foes that a friend should be the worst!

(v, 4, 62-72)

Not a single expression of concern for Silvia escapes his lips. She does not exist. *He*, Valentine, is the injured one. It is a sublime, a Balzacian expression of the ego. And his gesture of renunciation forms, if you like, a grotesque parody of Julia's quiet and undramatic forgiveness of Proteus. On the plane of romantic comedy, the magnitude of Valentine's ego demands comparison with Milton's Satan. The infallible good taste of Shakespeare renders silent the unfortunate Silvia, a word from whom would have sufficed to blow away the pretensions of the Big Production staged by Valentine and Proteus for their own benefit, and abetted by the Duke. The only reality-figure who is allowed a voice at the end—Thurio—very sensibly refuses to get hurt in the affair, and walks off to the hoots of the groundlings and the derision of those notable judges of human conduct, the Duke and Valentine. But Shakespeare's predilection for locating the common-sense viewpoint among clowns, boobies, and servants is already marked; and we should take, as the final internal criticism of the action, the words of Thurio: "I hold him but a fool that will endanger/His body for a girl that loves him not." (v, 4, 131-132)

III

I have concentrated in this analysis upon Valentine, because he embodies the central idea of the play—that is, the romantic conventions foundering, like capitalism in Marxist mythology, of inner contradictions. The ending of *Two Gentlemen* is self-evidently a refutation of the postures adopted by both young men in scene one. Strictly, no further refutation is required. But the romantic ideal, or illusion, if of course under fire from other quarters as well. It is attacked explicitly, by Speed; it is derided analogously, through the Launce-Crab infatuation. As everyone agrees, this relationship parodies (if rather heavy-handedly) the friendship and self-sacrifice

51

of the male leads.[5] And the Outlaws, too, supply their quota of satire. This mob of junior role players is sufficiently identified by the leader of their choice, Valentine. They are sketched in most economically. Valentine wins their hearts by his claim to have killed his man; whereupon they, anxious not to lose face, insist that they *too* have done desperate deeds. The point is that we know Valentine to be a liar, and therefore infer that the Outlaws are his mental siblings. Leader and led parallel, and implicitly criticize the other.

Nor is it necessary for the final page of the comedy to set the record straight. Critics frequently talk as if the attainment of self-knowledge is the major criterion of high-quality drama. Not at all. A perfectly legitimate alternative method, proper to comedy, is to allow a fair run to certain viewpoints, and then to suppress or gloss over them in the conclusion. It is sufficient for the audience—and not necessarily the principals—to have arrived at a proper view of the matter. Moreover, for all the principals to attain self-knowledge is surely to strain the bounds of comedy; the process is too painful. And so the self-satisfaction of the hero is in this play allowed to remain unpunctured. It is provocative, but it is legitimate. And the insufferable Valentine, as he departs patronizing everyone from the Duke downwards, is simply dramatizing a tautology of life: conventional behavior is applauded by the conventional.

[5] This concept is fully worked out in Harold F. Brooks, "Two Clowns in a Comedy (to say nothing of the Dog): Speed, Launce (and Crab) in *The Two Gentlemen of Verona*," *Essays and Studies 1963* (London, 1963), pp. 91-100.

To conclude, the fundamental critical error with *Two Gentlemen* is to take Valentine at his own evaluation as an attractive, appealing male lead. He is nothing of the sort. He is (and I gladly accept Charlton's term) a "nincompoop"; and this is the germ of the play, not an unsightly development forced on a tyro playwright by the exigencies of the conventions. I add that any reputable production of *Two Gentlemen* makes this clear. It can hardly be played in any other way; this comedy needs to be seen to be believed. For the rest, the play's center of sanity is placed unequivocally with the women. Silvia is necessarily a sketch only, but Julia is of the line that produces Portia and Viola. The play as a whole, which has very justly been termed Shakespeare's "laboratory," contains all the *parts* of a Shakespeare comedy; technically it is all there, and Shakespeare needed only to adjust the relation of the parts to the whole. That is, the idea of romance countered by realism, of folly raked by wisdom, achieves a more satisfying synthesis in the later plays. The Shakespearean system of internal checks and balances, developed to perfection in *As You Like It* and *Twelfth Night*, is essentially only a refinement of *Two Gentlemen*. And this play, finally, stakes out an area of concern that its author remains with throughout the comedies. It is illusion. The ironic coup of Valentine's renunciation is a masterly revelation of self-infatuation; the ending is illusion condoned. *Two Gentlemen*, like all the subsequent comedies, may make use of disguise; but the true focus is that for which disguise is but a figure, the world of illusion.

CHAPTER III

The Rules of the Game

The Taming of the Shrew, perhaps the most adroit of the early comedies, owes its perennial success on the boards to its synthesis of farce and comedy. The kernel of the play is, if one likes, a fairly brutal sex farce; the formula of man taming woman is one to agitate primitively the minds of all audiences. But the play contains also a subtle account of two intelligent people arriving at a modus vivendi. I do not mean by this that intelligent people will tend toward seeing the play as a robust comedy of manners, and the unintelligent as a roaring farce, though this may be true enough on occasion. I think rather that the archetypal action of *The Taming of the Shrew* is one to appeal to all minds, intelligent or not, and the emotions generated in the Katherina-Petruchio scenes form the substratum of a more sophisticated reaction to the piece. Clearly, a producer can have *The Taming of the Shrew* played for slapstick, without negating the text, and give innocent pleasure to many. But I propose here to say no more of the farce elements in the play, that is, the broadly comic aspects of Petruchio's wooing. I intend instead to examine the other play that Shakespeare has built up: the study of a single central relationship. Alone of the comedies, and virtually alone in the canon, *The Taming of the Shrew* concerns itself with such a relationship. If we set aside *Antony and Cleopatra* and perhaps *Romeo and Juliet*, no other play of Shakespeare's concentrates on a single relationship. This play is about Katherina and Petruchio, and the rest of the dramatis personae compose the backdrop to their relationship. *The Taming of the Shrew* advances ironically contrasted patterns of wooing, and at the heart of all, the rules of the game that husband and wife come to agree on.

I

We have first to dispose of the Induction. The Sly scenes raise considerable difficulties, though they are unquestionably from Shakespeare's hand. They have been persuasively defended by critics who see in them an extension of the play's theme of appearance and reality. The play acting to deceive Sly parallels the disguise motif in the main play; the supposedly dutiful wife matches Katherina, Bianca, and the Widow; the appearance-reality contrast describes the relationship between Katherina and Bianca, who in effect change places. All this is very convincing; but it does not explain the point of the Induction. The function of drama is not to dramatize themes, though it may at times appear so in the world of literary criticism. A theme is an abstraction, a means whereby a critic can profitably discuss a play; the play does not exist as a mere vehicle which serves, creaking and groaning, to trundle the Theme on to the boards. When, therefore, we are told that "the Induction . . . both succeeds in exploiting the overriding theme and in leading up to the play that follows it."[1] I ask: why "exploit" what is already *there*, and why lead up to what needs no leading up? The sentence tells us nothing about the dramatic point of the Induction. The trouble with writing "Sly's main function is to lead the spectator into the imaginary world of the play; and once he has done that, he is no longer required,"[2] is that it fails to identify the precise quality of *The Taming of the Shrew* that requires a lead-in. Virtually every other play in the canon manages without the apparatus of Induction Chorus; it just begins. There are clearly sound dramatic reasons for the Chorus in *Henry V* and *Pericles*. What makes *The Taming of the Shrew* a special case?

It would be different if the Sly scenes implied a judgment on the main comedy. But they don't. Nor can the play as a whole be reasonably regarded as a sustained meditation on reality and illusion, as *A Midsummer Night's Dream* can. Certainly *The Taming of the Shrew* makes full use of the contrast between reality and appearance, but then most comedies do. Take any major comedy at random—*Tartuffe, Arms and the Man, The School for Scandal*—and we can see that each exploits to some extent the opposition of appearance and reality. We can usefully think of that opposition less as a theme specific to a single play, than as an organic principle of much drama and most comedy. My point is that we ought

---

[1] E.M.W. Tillyard, *Shakespeare's Early Comedies* (London, 1965), pp. 105-106.

[2] G. R. Hibbard, in the New Penguin edn. of *The Taming of the Shrew* (Harmondsworth, England, 1968), p. 44.

not to invoke the theme of appearance and reality as a sufficient answer to the structural problem the Induction poses. I can see no way in which it is, dramatically, important to our understanding of the main comedy to have sat through the Induction first. The initial jest sets the mood for the play, but the whole strategy of a curtain raiser casts implicit doubts on the quality of the work to follow—doubts which *The Taming of the Shrew* in no way merits. It is a play perfectly capable of creating its own mood, and of explaining itself.

In fact, of course, the doubts that I have raised have been silently endorsed by a multitude of producers of *The Taming of the Shrew*; quite possibly—one can only guess—a literal majority of all those responsible for bringing the play on to the boards. In practice, producers do one of two important things to the text as it stands. First, they simply drop the Induction altogether, thus blasphemously truncating the theme of appearance and reality. Second, they retain the Induction, and play the additional Sly passages from *The Taming of a Shrew*. Authenticity aside, I am not altogether attracted to this solution, because it tends to give the main comedy the status of a wish-fulfillment dream in Sly's mind. The additional passages end:

Sly: Who's this? Tapster! O Lord, sirrah, I have had the bravest dream tonight that ever thou heardest in all thy life.

Tapster: Ay, marry, but you had best get you home, for your wife will course you for dreaming here tonight.

57

Sly: Will she? I know now how to tame a shrew. I
          dreamt upon it all this night till now, and thou
          hast waked me out of the best dream that ever
          I had in my life. But I'll to my wife presently,
          and tame her too an if she anger me.
Tapster: Nay tarry, Sly, for I'll go home with thee,
          And hear the rest that thou hast dreamt tonight.
                              Exeunt omnes

The realistic and psychologically convincing Katherina-
Petruchio scenes are not, I feel, best served by a framework that implies them to be a fantasy. Still, this solution
has an undeniable logic. And the continued interruptions
of Sly do provide a rather obvious opportunity for some
extra laughs (not that the play needs them).

In sum, I am not persuaded that I understand the point
of the Induction and its relationship to the play. I dislike critical solutions that postulate some reason of external necessity to account for some major problem in
the text; the critic's business in general is to make the
best of the text that, broadly, has come down to him, not
complain of its (and his) inadequacies. But here I feel
it necessary to conjecture some enigma of stage context,
some major textual subsidence, our knowledge of which
would give the Induction more point than it seems to
possess as it now stands. It may be, for instance, that the
pressures on the acting corps forced Shakespeare to cut
the scenes he had written for Sly (not necessarily, of
course, in the form that has survived in *A Shrew*). If,
say, Vincentio's part could only be filled at the expense
of Sly, then the later Sly passages would have to go. Or

perhaps Shakespeare simply revised his opinion of the effectiveness of the later interruptions. Some such conjecture seems a reasonable exit from the problems. But I cannot account for half-a-framework, or for an Induction that sets no scene, provides no comment, and creates a mood that the later play effortlessly generates for itself. I guess it to be a torso of Shakespeare's original plan, or the residue of a change of mind and theatrical circumstance.

II

The design of the main comedy is the pattern of wooings. Strictly, there are three. Hortensio and the Widow together underline a moral very clear elsewhere. He elects to marry a "wealthy widow," on the rebound from Bianca, within a brisk three days. Her main attraction, wealth aside, is her love for Hortensio. (IV, 2, 37-39) "Kindness in women, not their beauteous looks,/Shall win my love" he declares. (IV, 2, 41-42) It is an attitude fully refuted in the final scenes.

Hortensio and the Widow, however, form a miniature relationship. We are left with what is in effect a play composed of a double wooing action, Lucentio-Bianca and Petruchio-Katherina. The major and minor pairs execute a quadrille. Petruchio and Lucentio, though, while they stand in a significant relationship to each other in the play, have no personal relationship to speak of; the behavior of each man is unconditioned by the other, until the final scene. Now Katherina and Bianca have both a formal relationship, and an intense personal one.

59

Hence the situation that sets up the play, the situation that awaits Petruchio, consists essentially of Bianca, Katherina, and Lucentio.

If we take *The Taming of the Shrew* to follow *The Two Gentlemen of Verona*, Lucentio appears as the successor to Valentine; the posturing, conventional lover steps down from the lead role to that of foil to the realist hero, Petruchio. And Lucentio is the hunter-prey of Bianca. Bianca has no analogue in the early comedies, but is the minx to set off the shrew. This is not immediately plain; in the early scenes we have reasonable sympathies with Bianca and Lucentio. It is only later that the full ironic import of much of their dialogue comes home. The Lucentio-Bianca relationship not only parallels and contrasts with the major, it enables us to understand it. The inversion of sisters is the master movement of the play, their relationship with their lovers describing a chiasma; it is an instance of plot as motivation, for the existence of Bianca is the core of the soliloquy that Katherina never speaks.

Bianca's position in society, and in her father's affections, is based on apparent submissiveness and on silence. These qualities win such tributes as Lucentio's "this young modest girl" (I, 1, 153), and "But in the other's silence do I see/Maid's mild behavior and sobriety." (I, 1, 70-71) Similarly, Baptista's solicitude for his younger daughter: "And let it not displease thee, good Bianca,/For I will love thee ne'er the less, my girl." (I, 1, 76-77) Naturally enough, this evokes an explosion of rage from Katherina: "A pretty peat! it is best/Put finger in the

eye, an she knew why." (I, 1, 78-79) Bianca is play acting—a quality she continues to display throughout her
wooing by Lucentio—and Katherina knows it. Katherina's twin grievances are that the world vastly overvalues
her minx of a sister, and that she herself may be left
embarrassingly on the shelf. This is the burden of her
opening lines "I pray you sir, is it your will/To make a
stale of me amongst these mates?" (I, 1, 57-58), and of
the outburst of jealous rage at the favorite's place her
demure sister enjoys:

> Nay, now I see
> She is your treasure, she must have a husband;
> I must dance bare-foot on her wedding-day,
> And for your love to her lead apes in hell.
>
> (II, 1, 31-34)

It is fear, quite considerably justified, that leads Katherina to exaggerate her dislike of her sister and contempt
for her father. And quite possibly, as Petruchio asserts,
policy. While she continues in this shrewish vein, there is
no possibility that Baptista will dare permit the popular
Bianca to be married first. The contrived fury, as an instrument of policy, is well known in human relationship.
Its deployment here ensures an outcome that is, at least
up to a point, precisely as Katherina wishes. She is quite
intelligent enough to calculate the stimulus and its effect.

The tension between Katherina and Bianca places,
and accounts for, both of them. And we are enabled, at
least in retrospect, to perceive a further dimension of
each woman as the play progresses. Katherina, we can

61

see, is not purely a virago, but a woman with a case of sorts of whom something can be made. She has become part of a family behavior pattern in which all roles stimulate the others to exaggeration. Bianca's scenes gain in ironic weight. Their symbolic center is music. Bianca, we are told, "taketh most delight/In music, instruments, and poetry." (I, 1, 92-93) And music, symbol of harmony and order, serves neatly to distinguish the sisters. Katherina breaks Hortensio's lute across his head; Bianca's wooing proceeds on oiled wheels through the device of the music lesson. This scene, III, 1, is the key to the Bianca-Lucentio relationship. The point is that Lucentio and Hortensio, those two innocents, set up as teachers; and the subject of their instruction, music, yields Hortensio's fatuous tribute to Bianca, "the patroness of heavenly harmony." (III, 1, 5) Bianca will emerge in the final scene as the "rebel" (V, 2, 164), that is, opponent of order. Hence there is an inverted symbolism here that catches nicely the ironic force of the minor action. So, indeed, does the conclusion to the wedding scene:

Baptista: And let Bianca take her sister's room.
Tranio: Shall sweet Bianca practice how to bride it?
Baptista: She shall, Lucentio.

(III, 2, 246-248)

The move to Katherina's room typifies Shakespeare's symbolism of the unobtrusive, rather than emblematic, variety. The event alluded to is tiny, commonplace, prosaic; yet it represents the action of the play.

62

III

And so to the major action of the play, Petruchio's taming of Katherina. The nature of this action is very curiously caught, and typified, in Petruchio's initial appearance with Grumio: in the organism of a Shakespeare play, the part implies the whole. Petruchio enters with an order to his servant, "Here, sirrah Grumio, knock, I say." (I, 2, 5) Grumio affects to discover meanings other than the obvious in this simple injunction, whereupon Petruchio, rapidly losing patience, wrings Grumio by the ears to aid him to a better understanding of the matter. We see by this that Petruchio is a man of imperious will, and that his will extends to the interpretation of words. Words clear a path for Petruchio; he uses them either exactly, to disclose his plain intentions (as in his frank avowal to Hortensio, I, 2, 63-74), or eccentrically and hyperbolically, as in many of his dealings with Katherina. In both cases his words serve a thrusting and aggressive policy of will. In language as in action, Petruchio is the incarnation of the masculine.

He meets a worthy opponent in Katherina. Their encounter in II, 1 sets the pattern for the relationship: it is a magnificent rapier passage, the foils sliding and whirring as Petruchio seeks always to close while accepting a series of hits on the riposte. His opening breath is a thrust: "Good morrow, *Kate*." (II, 1, 182) With that word he bids for the mastery; the familiar diminutive is the privilege of the lord and master, and Katherina in insisting on *Katherine* fends off the presumptuous male.

63

Whereupon Petruchio—to whom words, if he owns them, have considerable importance—reiterates *Kate* no less than 11 times, and embarks on his planned strategy of misapplied hyperbole. It succeeds in disconcerting Katherina, for on hearing her virtues and mildness praised she can find nothing better than the "movable" jest. Thereupon they trade banter in the conventional mode, Petruchio's tending always to broad sexual innuendo, Katherina's toward demonstrating him a fool. The rules of this game are well established, and both show equal skill; but the rules include "hands-off," with a penalty clause. Thus, Petruchio makes several slightly oafish advances, which are duly punished. "Come, sit on me" (II, 1, 200) invites (and on the stage, likely gets) the short-arm jab. When Petruchio switches too broadly to sex—"tails" was a well-known joke-word—Katherina instantly breaks off: "Yours, if you talk of tails; and so farewell." (II, 1, 219)[3] There are limits, even on the Elizabethan stage; as Petruchio knows very well. Unable to prevent—such the speed of the fencing—the stock reference to an exotic sexual position, "What! with my tongue in your tail?" (II, 1, 220) Petruchio hastily retracts: "Nay, come again, good Kate, I am a gentleman." ("I am not the oaf you take me for.") This is to her departing back; there is no need for editors to insert here a stage direction, *He takes her in his arms*; the words suffice for the cuff that she roundly (and quite deservedly) administers him. The rules have been infringed. But Petruchio, breaking into the mode of direct statement, warns her of *his* understanding of the rules: "I swear I'll cuff you if you strike

[3] The spelling "tales" in line 219 robs the riposte of its point.

again." (II, 1, 223) The warning given, they resume their banter. It is worth noting that Petruchio keeps within the bounds of decency, and that Katherina does not strike him again. The point, on both sides, has been taken. It is all basically good humored. Petruchio's next attempt to close with her, naturally, meets with protest ("Let me go," II, 1, 243), but his smooth shift to hyperbole again baffles her: "No, not a whit. I find you passing gentle," etc. (II, 1, 244-258) This is distinctly on a higher level of maneuver than her part-amused, part-angry, part-puzzled rejoinder, "Go, fool, and whom thou keep'st command." (II, 1, 259) Petruchio has hit on the winning strategy; the policy of tongue-in-cheek hyperbole has no defense.

Except, of course, that of an identical policy. Katherina is for the moment reduced to asking questions as a form of marking time while she works out the counter-strategy: "Where did you study all this goodly speech?" (II, 1, 264) But not till her final speech in the play does she fully achieve this. For the moment, Petruchio's initiative carries all before him. He shifts to plain statement—his transitions are among his most effective tactics, "And therefore, setting all this chat aside,/Thus in plain terms" (II, 1, 270-271)—and announces his intent to wed. Katherina makes no immediate answer to his statement of intent; significantly, she addresses her protest to her father, whose convenient entrance absolves her from committal answer. Petruchio keeps up the pressure with a stream of jovial hyperbole—"Grissel" and "Lucrece" furnish comparisons—together with outrageous revelations of her sexual complaisance in private.

65

Yet the flow of nonsense yields disconcertingly to truth: the reiterated intent to wed, and the shrewd hit, "If she be curst, it is for policy." (II, 1, 294) It is all very baffling; Katherina doesn't know what to make of him. But the voice of protest is singularly small, and her sole retort to Petruchio, in company, is purely to save face: "I'll see thee hanged on Sunday first." (II, 1, 301) The fact is that Katherina likes him well enough. In sum, II, 1 reveals the foundations of a basic accord between the two. That accord is negotiated, rather than created, later. Both have a sense of the rules of the game; but Katherina has yet to penetrate Petruchio's strategy, and hence comprehend the terms of the marital games he intends to establish.

The wedding day defines the nature of their relationship much more precisely. It is not simply a contest for mastery as such, but a procedural dispute over the rules that are to govern their games. Each foresees the coming clash of wills, but prepares for it in different fashion. Katherina extracts all the advantage she can out of Petruchio's late, fantastical arrival at the church. For once, she actually gets some public sympathy:

Baptista: Go, girl, I cannot blame thee now to weep,
        For such an injury would vex a very saint,
        Much more a shrew of thy impatient humor.

                                    (III, 2, 27-29)

And she makes a perfectly reasonable request to her husband to delay his departure: "Let me entreat you." (III, 2, 196) Her strategy is to build up public opinion, based on her reasonableness, behind her. She intends to have "the law of our side." Petruchio's is a strategy of provocation. He intends to make her come out and fight, whereupon he will enforce the lord-and-master formula. It is a miniature Sumter-comedy; and Katherina, stung, fires the first shot: "Do what thou canst, I will not go today." (III, 2, 204) This gives Petruchio his opportunity:

I will be master of what is mine own.
She is my goods, my chattels; she is my house,
My household stuff, my field, my barn,
My horse, my ox, my ass, my anything;
(III, 2, 225-228)

The commentators whose liberal consciences are repelled by this outrageous declaration, miss its point, and Petruchio's customary mode of speech. It is a hyperbolic overstatement of male dominance, just as later Katherina is hyperbolically to assert female submissiveness. Petruchio is in effect saying that he will not brook contradiction in public, whatever the (quite deliberate) degree of provocation. The fencing for position has ended in Katherina's losing her temper, and thus exposing herself to a public rebuke.

Petruchio then proceeds with his plan. The servants, as usual, provide the shrewdest appraisal of the matter: "By this reck'ning he is more shrew than she" says Curtis (IV, 1, 74): "He kills her in her own humor" (IV, 1, 167) is Peter's version of the same point. The role reversal is underlined yet further by the key word "policy." Petruchio's earlier surmise that Katherina was "curst for policy" complements his soliloquy, "Thus have I politicly begun my reign." (IV, 1, 175-198) The process of forc-

ing her into submission is hastened by the curiously
modern tactic of starvation allied to deprivation of sleep;
and the episodes of the food, the tailor, and the time-
dialogue provide some of the broadest comedy of the
play.

That is, no doubt, the main purpose of those scenes;
Katherina is quite intelligent enough to have got the
point earlier. The point is finally established in IV, 5,
from which dates the understanding between the two.
Petruchio, in broad daylight, asserts "I say it is the moon
that shines so bright." (IV, 5, 4) And Katherina, after a
couple of incredulous contradictions, lets him have his
way. It is manifestly crazy, but if Petruchio wants it
so. . . . Her phrasing of the articles of capitulation is
exact:

> Then God be blessed, it is the blessèd sun,
> But sun it is not when you say it is not,
> And the moon changes even as your mind.
> What you will have it named, even that it is,
> And so it shall be still for Katherine.

> (IV, 5, 18-22)

It is a neat variant of the nominalist-realist argument.
Petruchio is accorded the masculine prerogative of nam-
ing things as he will (at least, in the marital context);
Katherina, the realist-woman, accepts the substance of
the matter. The form is that Petruchio, as Head of State,
has total command; the substance is that all other things
can be negotiated within that form. It is the true climax
of the comedy, as Hortensio sees at once: "Petruchio,

go thy ways, the field is won." (IV, 5, 23) The matter is put to a further test when they meet Vincentio, and here the future is plainly foreshadowed. Katherina, taking her cue from her husband, performs a sprightly volteface in greeting Vincentio first as a young gentlewoman, then as an old man. She does this not sullenly, but with perfect good humor; and her deployment of hyperbole shows that at last she has adopted Petruchio's mode: "Young budding virgin, fair and fresh, and sweet." (IV, 5, 37) She is now playing the same game as her husband. Her address to Vincentio marks not submission, but cooperation.

A further minor test occurs: the public kiss. "First kiss me, Kate." (V, 1, 130) A moment's hesitation, and it is granted. The accord is sealed. What follows, therefore, is not a true test, but a demonstration of that accord. It is a coda that recapitulates, clarifies, and emphasizes. The wedding feast serves, as is usual with Shakespearean feasts, to present a microcosm of a situation. The shrew still keeps her claws sharpened, but uses them on the widow—legitimately, for the widow starts the altercation. (The dialogue is wonderfully deft here: Shakespeare, always intent to trace the development of a situation to its conversational source, makes the argument flow naturally from Petruchio's innocent "Padua affords nothing but what is kind." (V, 2, 14) And so we come to the challenge, Baptista's recognition of metamorphosis, "Another dowry to another daughter,/For she is changed as she had never been," (V, 2, 119-120) and Katherina's final speech. Shaw found it "altogether

69

disgusting to modern sensibility,"[4] and one can see his point. But we really cannot take that speech at face value. Much of this comedy is an unspoken dialogue between Katherina and Petruchio; and we have to take her speech in the context of the whole play, not as a set-piece on the woman's place. We should read Katherina's final speech as the parallel, and answer, to Petruchio's rhetoric. The mode of speech adopted by each is hyperbole. We need not argue the content, but a modified version of the hyperbole—the notion that males adopt a formal lead, and initiative, in matters involving both sexes—still exists, if only in ritual form, in our day. In other words Katherina, like her husband, is merely overstating an essential truth. Psychologically, her homily to the Widow and Bianca is perfectly apt. Katherina, laying it on with a trowel, is cooperating fully with her husband to despoil the neighbors. This is a husband-wife team that has settled, to its own satisfaction, the rules of its games, and now preaches them unctuously to its friends.

Katherina's speech, therefore, is Euclidean in its reduction of the play's design. It would be *simpliste* to regard this statement of total passivity at its face value, and as a prognosis. The open end of *The Taming of the Shrew* is Katherina's mind, undisclosed in soliloquy. And so it is appropriate that the play should end on a faint, but ominous, question mark.

Hortensio: Now, go thy ways, thou hast tamed a curst
　　　　shrew.

[4] *Shaw on Shakespeare*, ed. Edwin Wilson (London, 1962), p. 180.

Lucentio: 'Tis a wonder, by your leave, she will be
            tamèd so.

(*Exeunt*)

We have had small reason to respect the soundness of Lucentio's judgment. He is not in the first flight of choric voices. Still, Lucentio has had some hard times lately; and he is learning.

CHAPTER IV

The Words of Mercury

Love's Labour's Lost is probably better appreciated today than at any time since its earliest performances. It is now found to play well, and it has had some extremely understanding criticism over the last two decades. Nowadays critics have slackened their efforts to expound the play as a sophisticated in-joke, a spoof on Lyly and on the School of Night. No doubt it is all that, but the concentration on the topical interest of *Love's Labour's Lost* tended to obscure its permanent value. The play retains its elusiveness, but is today generally regarded as a delicate and controlled movement toward an acceptance of reality. "Reality" is a term that (however unsatisfactory philosophically) critics agree upon as a convenient designation for the target of the play's probing.[1] The word is not susceptible to exact definition, but it designates all

[1] Thus Bobbyann Roesen generally in "Love's Labour's Lost," *Shakespeare Quarterly*, IV (1953), 411-426. A. C. Hamilton writes that "a reality does lie beneath the surface," *The Early Shakespeare* (San Marino, California, 1967), p. 139. Marco Mincoff sees the death of the King as "a breath of stark reality against which to measure the artificiality of the courtly game of love," "Shakespeare and Lyly," *Shakespeare Survey 14* (Cambridge, 1961), p. 20. And Philip Parsons views the later stages of the play as "this intangible movement toward reality," "Shakespeare and the Mask," *Shakespeare Survey 16* (Cambridge, 1963), p. 123.

those phenomena of life that are symbolized by the entry of Mercade. That entry is the key fact of the play: it is hardly possible to sustain the argument that it is "sudden, unprovided for, external to the inner necessity of the plot, and for that reason aesthetically unsatisfactory, though theatrically effective."[2] For the play has opened with an assault upon Time/Death (lines 1-14), as it closes with the acknowledgment of Time's victory. The death message is organically present in Scene 1, as certain cells die shortly after the body's birth. And the final Act makes sense only as a reversal of the first Act: the themes of light-darkness, folly-wisdom, fantasy-reality are initiated and resolved in the exposition and conclusion.

The "movement toward reality" is a perfectly valid way of describing the form of the play; it is, I believe, the best way of describing what *happens* in *Love's Labour's Lost*. And we can as readily see it as a set of reversals, refutations of the untenable positions taken up in Act I—just as, perhaps, the logic of the final Wintersong refutes Summer. But I want here to examine the form of *Love's Labour's Lost*, not as a temporal process, but as an evolving analysis of humanity's primary symbol for reality: words. Commentators have fastened on the word-play in *Love's Labour's Lost*, and have, I believe, missed that the play is about *words*. Words compose the central symbol of *Love's Labour's Lost*;[3] it is

---

[2] Peter G. Phialas, *Shakespeare's Romantic Comedies: The Development of Their Form and Meaning* (Chapel Hill, North Carolina, 1966), p. 99.

[3] Hamilton, *op.cit.*, pp. 129-131, has noted the many occasions when "word" is alluded to. In fact, "word" (and its plural) oc-

toward this symbol that the characters are oriented; it is through it that they define themselves. I do not mean by this that "the contrast of different characters in terms of their different idiom, played off or chiming together, constitutes the 'form' of the comedy," as M. C. Bradbrook puts it.[4] Obviously, the play contains a number of contrasting idioms, and a very considerable part of its delight lies in the virtuosity with which these idioms are exploited and counterpointed. But the play's central principle of organization creates groupings which are broader than the individual idioms in them. In essence, then, I see the dramatis personae in *Love's Labour's Lost* as falling into four main groups, characterized by different attitudes toward words; and the interaction of these groups sets up an intellectual drama that underlies the emotional and personal conflicts.

I

Navarre, Berowne, Dumain, and Longaville are equivocators. They are concerned with two sorts of words; words as jests, words as oaths. But they do not distinguish absolutely between the two categories; it is a very great error, for an oath cannot exist in the context of a jest, nor a jest in an oath. Essentially, they undermine

---

curs 48 times. The statistics for the other plays written at this period provide a suggestive comparison: there are 17 references in *The Comedy of Errors*; 25, in *The Taming of the Shrew*; 29, in *The Two Gentlemen of Verona*; and 13, in *A Midsummer Night's Dream*. The three parts of *Henry VI* have 23, 34, and 39, with 9 in *Richard III*.

[4] M. C. Bradbrook, *Shakespeare and Elizabethan Poetry* (London, 1951), p. 215.

words, for they see words as projections of their personal whims. The occasion that serves to expose their abuse of words is a fantastic "study"-project manifestly opposed to "common sense" (I, 1, 47)—a term with a meaning very similar to ours. It is a denial of reality shared by all four. We need not pursue minor distinctions down to the Dumain-Longaville level (though this is possible), but the King and Berowne offer different aspects of the matter.

Navarre has the imperial tendency to want words to match his wishes. Words are his servants. There is a slight, but unmistakable, touch of oafishness about him; a favorite word of his is "chat"; thus, to Rosaline: "If you deny to dance, let's hold more chat," (v, 2, 229) and, more plainly:

> Are we not all in love? . . .
> Then leave this chat; and, good Berowne, now prove
> Our loving lawful and our faith not torn.
> (IV, 3, 277, 279-280)

It is the eternal voice of the superior officer, dismissing with a disdainful monosyllable some business that he does not comprehend, and leaving it to a clever second-in-command to arrange. "Chat" is the utterance of a man who does not understand words, and does not respect them. Navarre is responsible for the play's most embarrassing moment, when—following the news of the death—he tries, with unbelievable lack of sensibility, to keep the old game going: "The extreme parts of time extremely forms," and so on through a threadbare string of conceits. (v, 2, 730-41) It asks for, and gets, the

75

ultimate blank wall of language: "I understand you not."
(v, 2, 742) His penance will instruct him that words—
as oaths—have a meaning and status that lie outside his
authority.

Berowne is, however, the focus of the word-attitudes
current in his group. He is not deceived by words: he
has an ironic appreciation of all modes of language, and
can switch easily from plain to tuppence-colored. He is
vitiated by a fundamental lack of faith in words as counters; the jest devalues all currency. When we first encounter him he is trying to back out of an oath, his
agreement to study for three years on the King's terms,
which seems likely to prove uncomfortable: "By yea and
nay, sir, then I swore in jest." (i, 1, 54) Already he
erodes the status of words as oaths. But he is distinguished from the first scene onwards by a highly equivo-
cal attitude to words. "Necessity will make us all forsworn," he warns prophetically (i, 1, 148): an attitude
which the course of the play refutes. The trouble with
Berowne is very clearly stated in the exchange between
Margaret and Boyet:

Margaret: Not a word with him but a jest.
Boyet: And every jest but a word.
(ii, 1, 214)

Boyet's comment is a covert reproach, and a most important one. For Berowne's attack upon the integrity of
words leads him to a dilemma, which he himself sees
clearly: "Let us once lose our oaths to find ourselves,/
Or else we lose ourselves to keep our oaths." (iv, 3, 356-

357) So the reality principle asserts itself, forcing Berowne to reexamine the bases of his course of conduct. But even though Berowne talks sense, in his praise of love (IV, 3, 284-360), his ready volte-face betrays the true weakness; he accords too little fixed value to words. He has betrayed an oath, and the frivolity of that original oath is itself the fault. The reality principle is revealed in the language, a sudden shift to Longaville's "Now to plain-dealing—lay these glozes by." (IV, 3, 365) And Berowne's "Allons! Allons! Sowed cockle reaped no corn;/And justice always whirls in equal measure," (IV, 3, 378-379) is an ominous hint of retribution, recalling the earlier remark of Longaville: "He weeds the corn, and still lets grow the weeding." (I, 1, 96) Here, too, the pattern of ironic reversal holds good. Berowne's fate is to have the true meaning of "jest" painfully instilled into him. We can pass over the oft-quoted rejection of "Taffeta phrases" in favor of "russet yeas and honest kersey noes" (V, 2, 403-414): it is a jesting confession, an adroit attempt to wriggle out of an insupportable situation and, in context, cannot be taken at its face value. The end, for Berowne, comes when he has to swear *in earnest* to jest—a nice reversal of the opening scene, and a fitting punishment for his besetting vice.

In sum, the King and Berowne typify in their different ways two modes of abusing words. The King wants words to mean what he wants them to mean; Berowne has the opposite tendency, the star debater's readiness to deploy words in any cause, for or against. Willfulness in one case, frivolity in the other, is the fault. Their

common penance is to learn the meaning of oaths, hence
of words in general, and to see reasserted their status as
symbols of reality.

II

The Princess and her court have, for all their gaiety,
the utmost respect for words as symbols of reality.
"Through them, in some sense, the voice of Reality
speaks," as Miss Roesen remarks.[5] The values of the
court are concentrated in its mistress, and we can readily
arrive at them by examining the Princess's words. She
announces them with her opening lines:

> Good Lord Boyet, my beauty, though but mean,
> Needs not the painted flourish of your praise:
> Beauty is bought by judgment of the eye,
> Not uttered by base sale of chapmen's tongues.

> (II, 1, 13-16)

The Princess, gracious and shrewd, stands for sound
values arrived at by the senses; and she is utterly opposed
to meaningless words. Shortly after, she engages in a pro-
longed colloquy with Navarre. It centers first on oath
breaking (II, 1, 96-105) as a largely theoretic matter,
then moves to a discussion of words as pacts, that is to
say of oaths in the political sphere. This episode, which
puzzled Tillyard,[6] seems at first sight something of an
irrelevance. We can, however, justify the legal business
(II, 1, 127-166) as a variant on the theme of oath keep-

---

[5] Roesen, op.cit., p. 415.
[6] E.M.W. Tillyard, *Shakespeare's Early Comedies* (London,
1965), p. 153.

ing. It figures the main affair of *Love's Labour's Lost*, the status of words; and the Princess is quick to accord the full value to words, if possible: "We arrest your word" (ɪɪ, 1, 158)—that is, "seize your word as security." It is surely a reminder of the crucial position of words in the world of affairs; that the world as we know it functions on agreements that must if possible be maintained.

The Princess figures in another episode of prime importance. In ɪv, 1, she rewards the Forester for wittily telling the truth: "Here, good my glass, take this for telling true—" (ɪv, 1, 18): a testimony to the importance she attaches to true words. And her speech on the deer (ɪv, 1, 21-35) is not only a sudden shift of mood, a glimpse into a deeper play; it is also the thematic counter to the King's opening speech in praise of "fame." For the Princess (moving from the deer example, Hamlet-like, to the real point) says:

> And out of question so it is sometimes,
> Glory grows guilty of detested crimes,
> When, for fame's sake, for praise, an outward part,
> We bend to that the working of the heart;
> As I for praise alone now seek to spill
> The poor deer's blood, that my heart means no ill.
> (ɪv, 1, 30-35)

Fame, for the Princess, is merely an incitement to unnatural and pain-bringing activity. So it turns out for Navarre and his court, too; but the Princess has said it. She is beyond question the internal arbiter of the values of *Love's Labour's Lost*.

The Princess is seen at her most commanding in the final Act. Her attitude to words is expressed decisively in her comment on the badinage of Katherine and Rosaline: "Well bandied both; a set of wit well played." (v, 2, 29) The metaphor is central, and exact. The Princess and her retinue see words as *games*.[7] This is not at all the same thing as jests. They may indeed make jests, but they never devalue words. The "game" metaphor implies rules, scrupulously observed by all participants in the contest. The women in *Love's Labour's Lost* use words, but are never used by them.

When, therefore, the women come into contact, and therefore conflict, with the men, they are only superficially sharing the same idiom. In reality, two different modes of language are in collision. The feminine objective is to unmask the *meaning* of the words, that is, to relate words to the motives and purposes of the originators. The poems they regard as "a huge translation of hypocrisy." (v, 2, 51) As for the Russian masquerade, the Princess counters this with an unmasking device:

> The effect of my intent is to cross theirs.
> They do it but in mockery merriment,
> And mock for mock is only my intent.
>
> (v, 2, 138-140)

The women will play according to their own rules and on ground of their own choosing:

[7] C. L. Barber, in *Shakespeare's Festive Comedy* (Princeton, 1959), p. 95, notes that the word-play is associated with various sports and games—tilting, duelling, tennis, dice.

80

Rosaline: If they do speak our language, 'tis our will
　　　That some plain man recount their purposes.
　　　　　　　　　　　　(v, 2, 176-177)

And, in the interrogation that follows, the conceit ("we
have measured many miles/To tread a measure with
her on this grass," v, 2, 185-186) yields to the ruthless
application of the reality principle. This passage—conceit exposed by reality—is basic to the whole play.

The Princess's court—and one can legitimately include the epicene Boyet in the group—upholds the value
of truth, or reality. The women reason like philosophers.
They use words to establish the meaning of words, and
hence to relate words to the intentions of the men. This
not only accords with their sexual function—the word
game is more serious for women—it expresses an intellectual role, women as realists, that we can see elsewhere
in Shakespeare. At all events, they play the word game
with an essentially serious skill that deservedly puts the
men to shame.

III

The clowns, Costard and Dull (with whom one can
associate Moth) are the lower-class equivalent of the
women. They, too, are realists of the first order. Within
the limits of their education and intelligence, they are
not to be deceived. The prime assumption of Costard
and Dull is that words symbolize things. (This, be it
noted, is a more rudimentary phase of the inquiry initiated by the women, into words as symbols of motives.)

Costard, the "rational hind," is certainly a reality-man. Note his reply to the charge brought against him by Armado: "Sir, I confess the wench." (I, 1, 268) The words of Armado are not for him, and his own words express a *fact*. Costard, like Moth (and Feste) knows that money is a form of reality. His brief cadenza on "remuneration" (III, 1, 127-133) shows that he is not deceived; words have to symbolize things, and he is aware of their relationship. He is quite clear that one remuneration equals three farthings, and one guerdon equals a shilling, and he has a sardonic awareness—confirmed by Berowne—that a remuneration, in spite of its opulent aura, buys only three-farthings worth of silk. (III, 1, 135-140) To Costard, fittingly, are given the words that shortly precede the entry of Mercade: "she's quick; the child brags in her belly already. 'Tis yours." (V, 2, 666-667) The language, staccato and decisive, prefigures the reality that is shortly to blow the pageant away.

Dull shares Costard's position on words. He is in accord with the view that words must symbolize things. For him, a pricket is a pricket, and not a *haud credo*. (IV, 2, 12-21) The triangular discourse with Holofernes and Sir Nathaniel reveals Dull at his best, stubbornly holding his own; he is like a bridge player, refusing to be psyched out of his hand. And we have the exquisite pleasure of seeing in that scene one of the play's realists patronized by the pedants. "Sir, he hath never fed of the dainties that are bred in a book," as Sir Nathaniel observes. (IV, 2, 23) But Dull, not to be put down, has the audacity to try on an ancient riddle. And while his adversaries are dealing with this sudden counterattack, he clinches the engagement with a return to his original point: "and I say beside that, 'twas a pricket that the princess killed." (IV, 2, 45-46) It is worth noting that for all the word play, the three are actually discussing a *fact*, i.e., what sort of deer the Princess shot—buck or pricket. These three are by no means such fools as they look, and emerge well from a comparison with their (male) social superiors.

The clowns, then, form a natural alliance with the ladies. They are intellectual, if not social, complements. (A pairing later to be refined to Viola and Feste.) In the great work of determining the status of words, the clowns undertake the primary task: that of establishing the relationship between words and things. Without it no progress at all is possible. And we can, I think, comprehend the importance Shakespeare assigns to the clowns' role by noting the parallelism he supplies between the Princess and Dull. Both of them use words honestly, and both are ready to admit when words have failed to communicate:

Dull: Nor understand none neither, sir.

                                          (v, 1, 137)

Princess: I understand you not.   (v, 2, 742)

IV

Armado, Holofernes, and Nathaniel complete the spectrum of attitudes. They are concerned with words as things in themselves, rather than as symbols for other realities. Such an attitude can be dangerous, if indulged too far; and for Armado it is part of his incessant role

83

playing. His role as prototype of the dandy requires him to flourish words like ruffles. Since words are the mode, he uses them modishly: "A man of fire-new words, fashion's own knight" (I, 1, 175), as Berowne remarks. In his way, his circumlocutions form another denial of reality. This situation is confirmed by his incapacity at numbers: "I am ill at reckoning; it fitteth the spirit of a tapster." (I, 2, 39) (In *Love's Labour's Lost*, money and mathematics are infallible symbols of reality. The clowns—see, for example, Costard, v, 2, 491-500—never err in primary arithmetic.) It is impossible to determine whether his impulse toward Jacquenetta is a genuine yielding to reality, or a decision to incorporate her into his role playing. He, too, goes the way of Navarre and company: "I shall be forsworn (which is a great argument of falsehood) if I love" (I, 2, 157-158)—and therefore constitutes a variant of their error. But while the others, at the end, see their roles shattered by reality, Armado contrives to incorporate reality into his role. The three-year penance at the plough, clearly, suits him psychologically very well. He is a disturbing testimony to the importance of words as adjuncts to one man's reality.

We can dispose of Moth in relation to Armado, though he properly belongs with the clowns. Moth, in his scene with Armado (I, 2) is only apparently playing the same word game. Actually, he is a better educated version of Costard; he knows precisely what words relate to. He tells his master scornfully that the three-year study project is a mere infatuation with words. (I, 2, 36-52) He has no opinion of the quality of Armado's love: "Most maculate thoughts, master, are masked under such colors." (I, 2, 87-88) And again, he refers his sense of reality to the monetary standard I suggested earlier:

Armado: How hast thou purchased this experience?
Moth: By my penny of observation.

(III, 1, 23-24)

With Moth, as with the others, a man is known by the metaphors he keeps.

And there is Holofernes. He has had a bad Press—Dover Wilson, for example, sees him as "the eternal type of pedant, the 'living-dead man' who will always be with us, because so long as there is a human race to be educated there will always be many to mistake the letter for the spirit."[8] But there is a case to be made for him. Holofernes is animated by a pure, intense love of words for their own sake. It is a disinterested passion, and he admits it readily:

This is a gift that I have, simple, simple; a foolish extravagant spirit, full of forms, figures, shapes, objects, ideas, apprehensions, motions, revolutions. These are begot in the ventricle of memory, nourished in the womb of pia mater, and delivered upon the mellowing of occasion. But the gift is good in those in whom it is acute, and I am thankful for it.

(IV, 2, 63-69)

Predictably, he does not care for Armado, one of his own tribe (no more does Armado care for him, v, 2, 526-527), and provides an epitome for the two of them

[8] John Dover Wilson, *Shakespeare's Happy Comedies* (London, 1962), pp. 73-74.

85

(plus the attendant Sir Nathaniel): "He is too picked, too spruce, too affected, too odd, as it were, too peregrinate, as I may call it." (v, 1, 12-15) This is a great joy for all of us. But Holofernes is not a fool. He is addicted to verbal arabesques, but this harmless enough. They do not interfere with his sense of reality—he functions perfectly well in the limited society which is his normal milieu. He is, in his scene with Dull and Sir Nathaniel, discussing a fact—one of specialist interest only, to be sure, but a fact nonetheless. And he does not come to grief at the end. His merciless ragging by Berowne and company expresses them, but leaves him, though "out of countenance," with his essential dignity unshaken. He has a superb final line, in equal command of English and the situation: "This is not generous, not gentle, not humble." (v, 2, 621) He has to retire, but the inner man is undefeated. Holofernes' love of words for their own sake is a faculty that Shakespeare—as well he might—treats gently enough here.

Through this grouping of the characters in *Love's Labour's Lost* we can study the intellectual center of the play: words. *Love's Labour's Lost* is a sustained inquiry into the nature and status of words; and the characters in it embody, define, and implicitly criticize certain concepts of words. Shifting patterns of speakers endlessly debate the propositions, establishing or seeing refuted their word concepts. The main concepts are these: first, words as jests. Ultimately, this can be a way of rejecting reality—an attempted statement that it is not so. So, though words can be used gaily, they must themselves be treated seriously. The play presents right and wrong models. Those who wish to jest must, like the Princess, use words as in games—that is, adhering strictly to the rules of usage. One must never jest by oath breaking. An oath is sacred, for it is a wholly laudable attempt to invest words with meaning by submitting policies and actions to the agreed mediation of words. Navarre and his courtiers, then, see their confusion between "oaths" and "jests" refuted by events—and by the ladies. Words as symbols for things is a concept stoutly upheld by the clown-realists, who emerge unscathed from the play; their mission is humble, but absolutely necessary. And finally, words as things in themselves is a concept delicately criticized in Armado; they become a part of his role, to the extent that they exclude an awareness of reality. But the concept is allowed to pass with Holofernes, who, whatever his other faults, has his passion for words under control. The pressures of reality test, but do not refute, Holofernes.

And reality is the test to which all the characters must submit. It is there, throughout the play, waiting for them; it begins to throb like a pulse in the last scene, well before Mercade enters. Reality is hinted at by the three-by-three dialogue between Berowne and Costard (v, 2, 487-495): more strongly by the baiting (Malvolio-like) of Holofernes ("A light for Monsieur Judas! it grows dark, he may stumble," 622); and the Princess's Olivia-like consolation, "Alas! poor Maccabaeus, how hath he been baited" (623); Dumain seems to sense its implications as he cries, "Though my mocks come home by me, I will now be merry" (626-627); then Armado's "The

87

sweet war-man is dead and rotten" (652); Costard's rasping "she's quick; the child brags in her belly already. 'Tis yours" (666-667). The beat grows louder and more insistent, as the combatants square up, then Mercade enters.

He, Mercade-Mercury, is the messenger of the gods, bringing the tidings of mortality. His words dissolve the world of illusion and announce the presence of a reality that must be mediated by words. Armado is the first to see it, and his language is itself a rite of confession: "For mine own part, I breathe free breath. I have seen the day of wrong through the little hole of discretion, and I will right myself like a soldier." (v, 2, 713-715) Then the King is rebuked into using "honest plain words"; and Berowne, the core of the King's party, has to endure the play's central penance. *Words* are the means whereby Berowne is to pass his purgatory, his initiation into the world of reality. His penance sets jokes to work; it restores the meaning of oaths, hence of words, and reasserts their status as symbols of reality. That is the main point established by the close of *Love's Labour's Lost*. And the final songs, perhaps, take up the hint dropped by Armado in Act III; "it is an epilogue, or discourse to make plain/Some obscure precedence that hath tofore been sain." (III, 1, 74-75) The burden of that epilogue is plain enough. Summer and Winter are both aspects of reality; but Winter is second, and final. The season of death ends the play, as the news of death had stilled the Worthies. It is the final message from the forces that govern the pageant. "The words of Mercury are harsh after the songs of Apollo."

CHAPTER V

The Dream and the Play

Compared with the earlier comedies, *A Midsummer Night's Dream* represents a kind of dramatized synecdoche, an expansion of the emblematic parts into the whole. The technique of crystallizing the idea of the play into certain crucial symbolic passages (e.g., the "idol" passages in *Two Gentlemen of Verona*, II, 4; IV, 2; IV, 4, and the masque episode in *Love's Labour's Lost*, V, 2) is here intensified. *A Midsummer Night's Dream* is, in effect, nothing but two dramatized symbols: the dream, and the play.[1] In this, the comedy shows itself to be quintessentially baroque in its preoccupations.[2] For baroque thought is fascinated with the twin metaphors of life as a dream, and the world as a stage; and baroque drama, as with Bernini and Calderon,[3] not only explores these metaphors in dramatic form, but is fascinated by

---

[1] "In *A Midsummer Night's Dream*, romance merges into symbolist drama." S. C. Sen Gupta, *Shakespearian Comedy* (Oxford/Calcutta, 1950), p. 62.

[2] Early, or pre-baroque, according to one's dating of the period. I am content with the conventional date assigned to the beginnings of baroque, c. 1600, but clearly one has to recognize the anticipations of baroque that begin to appear in the 1590's.

[3] See Calderon's *Life Is a Dream*, and the account of Bernini's illusionist entertainment in Richard Bernheimer's "Theatrum Mundi," in *The Art Bulletin*, XXXVIII, 225-247.

the techniques and psychology of illusion. "Illusion" is, in fact, the term best adapted to describe the theme of *A Midsummer Night's Dream*. It covers the grand subjectivities of the lovers' relationships, and the incompetent illusionist techniques of the players. The two other elements of the play—Theseus, with Hippolyta, and the fairies—have primarily the status of frame, and instrument, of the action. They provide the scaffolding within which *A Midsummer Night's Dream* can be played out.

I

Theseus opens, as he closes, the play's action. His opening words contain the initial invocation to the moon, which as all agree is the unifying symbol for the action. Constantly alluded to (there are 30 references in all) the moon is an appropriate figure for fantasy, perhaps for transformation. But Theseus' role is much more important than that of master of ceremonies to the play. He provides the frame of reason for the subjectivities of the principals. His utterances are cool, mature, adult. The point is worth emphasizing, for although everyone quotes his later speech on "the lunatic, the lover, and the poet," the same approval is normally withheld from the line Theseus takes in scene one. The idea of an arranged marriage, with death as the ultimate sanction, is so monstrous to a modern reader that one tends to reject automatically, or accept purely as a donnée of the plot, Theseus' support for Egeus. But this is not how it would necessarily appear to an Elizabethan audience,[4] nor is it

[4] In the course of an address delivered at the M.L.A. meetings

Shakespeare's intention to present the matter unequivocally in that light. Of course the ancient Athenian edict invoking the death penalty is, as we should say, a barbarous survival. It is, however, merely touched on by Theseus—it is not a ruler's business to decry the laws of his realm—and he elaborates on exile to a nunnery as the likelier penalty for disobedience to a father's will. For what is the sum of Egeus' complaint? That his daughter has been "bewitched" by Lysander, and now spurns his own choice, Demetrius. "Bewitched" is not a bad description for the act of falling in love, as the course of the play demonstrates. Theseus strongly recommends the path of filial obedience to Hermia, and their crucial exchange introduces the eye motif which is the true iterative image of *A Midsummer Night's Dream*:

Hermia: I would my father looked but with my eyes.
Theseus: Rather your eyes must with his judgment look.
(I, 1, 56-57)

Reason stands by cool judgment; love, by pure subjectivity, for the "eye" in this comedy is a channel of passion as well as an organ of perception. Theseus' very sane advice to Hermia is to accept her father's judgment in the matter of marriage. There is, however, a strong hint that he is prepared to urge a more flexible line in private, once the public stand has been taken.

---

in 1967 in Chicago, Dr. James G. McManaway remarked that a prolonged study of a cache of Elizabethan social documents had left him with one overriding impression: that the average audience of *Romeo and Juliet* would have regarded the behavior of the young lovers as deserving everything they got.

Theseus: But Demetrius, come,
      And come, Egeus. You shall go with me;
      I have some private schooling for you both.
      For you, fair Hermia, look you arm yourself
      To fit your fancies to your father's will;
      Or else the law of Athens yields you up
      (Which by no means we may extenuate)
      To death, or to a vow of single life.
      Come, my Hippolyta. What cheer, my love?
      Demetrius and Egeus, go along.
      I must employ you in some business
      Against our nuptial and confer with you
      Of something nearly that concerns yourselves.

                        (I, 1, 114-126)

The Janus face of Theseus—strong for the laws in public, ready to try techniques of conciliation in private—is of a piece with the poise of the play. (Hippolyta, it seems, is troubled about the matter, hence Theseus repeats and elaborates the commands of the first three lines. He is reassuring Hippolyta; but the lovers fail to pick up the hint, intent as usual on their own emotions.) I do not suggest that the Egeus-Theseus view of the lovers is the right one, merely that it is an indispensable element in the play. In view of the conclusion to the night's activities—Egeus' choice, Demetrius, has to be doped out of love for Hermia, and Lysander into love for her, a state of affairs apparently perfectly satisfactory to all parties—can one confidently assert that Egeus is a tyrannical old fool, and that Theseus is wrong to support his judgment?

Without Theseus, there is no frame of values. Without the fairies, there is no action. The Oberon-Titania altercation, its necessity to the plot apart, sketches in perhaps a brief account of the aftermath of marriage, the climax to love-madness. Mutually jealous, Oberon and Titania bandy discreetly phrased charges of excessive passion for Theseus and Hippolyta. The moon, for Titania, is a symbol for disorder, "governess of floods." (II, 1, 103) Disorder thus counterpoints error and illusion; and the moon presides over all these aspects of human, and fairy, interaction. Out of the contention between Oberon and Titania grows the plan to engineer disorder; and Puck is the chosen instrument for the device. A natural agent of error, first introduced as "Robin Goodfellow," he has a long record of successful tricks. His orders are to drop the juice of "love-in-idleness" upon the eyes of Titania and the scornful Demetrius. The dramatic point of the juice is that it simulates, and therefore parodies, the conditions of love. It may involve Titania in what Oberon calls "hateful fantasies" (II, 1, 258); but the language in which she, and the others affected, protest their rapture is indistinguishable from that in which the unjuiced proclaim their love. The potion that Puck is ordered to drop into others' eyes is more than a mere device for inducing error, it is a delicately humorous symbol for love itself.

II

The real play now begins; it is the exploration of the play's title, and the dramatization of the proposition that

93

love is a dream. Strictly, the title contains more than one symbol. Anne Righter well remarks that night, sleep, shadows, and dreams are all symbols of illusion.[5] I take "dream" to be the central one of the cluster, however. It is seen as a condition of illusion induced by the operation of the love-juice, and the symbolic relations point to the view we are intended to take of the main action.

A Midsummer Night's Dream is in the first place an account of the relations between a quartet of young lovers. Critics have legitimately protested that it is hard to distinguish between them; but this is transparently a part of Shakespeare's design. This is, perhaps, one of the very few episodes in Shakespeare in which readers may find it helpful rather than insulting to be offered a résumé of the action. The relations between the four lovers pass through these stages:

(i) Hermia and Lysander love each other; Demetrius loves Hermia and despises Helena, who loves him.

(ii) Following the application of the love-juice, Lysander wakes believing he loves Helena.

(iii) Demetrius wakes, believing he loves Helena.

(iv) They battle over Helena, as they earlier did over Hermia.

(v) Lysander is given the juice-antidote, hence returns to Hermia.

(vi) Demetrius is not given the antidote, hence remains in love with Helena.

A bare recital of the events makes its own comments.

[5] Anne Righter, *Shakespeare and the Idea of the Play* (London, 1962), p. 106.

The irony engenders itself. And it is perfectly clear in the text, for Oberon himself describes the antidote as having the power "To take from thence all error with his might" (III, 2, 368), from which a sufficient judgment on Demetrius' final—and convenient—position may be inferred.

Shakespeare's design is to present a quartet of young people who (man for man, woman for woman) are virtually interchangeable. The physical differences (and some psychological) between Hermia and Helena provide some comic business, and help the actresses to realize their parts, but essentially they remain within the same categories. The only important distinction is between male and female. The men are enthusiastic captives of their own desires and rationalizations; Demetrius especially, that "spotted and inconstant man," is a descendant of Proteus. The women, as is customary in Shakespeare, are depicted as constant in love, and somewhat more adult and intelligent than their male counterparts. But this is not to say too much for them. The level of thought of all four is conventional; the banal and stilted quality of the lovers' lines is an index of their immature and conventional minds.[6] The primary image through which Shakespeare analyzes their relationships is that of the eye. "Eye" is easily the main motif in *A Midsummer Night's Dream*; it occurs in that form 20 times, and in compounds and plurals a further 48 times.

---

[6] Shakespeare uses this device frequently in the comedies. As late as *Much Ado About Nothing*, for example, Beatrice uses (for her) quite unworthily stilted verse on overhearing that Benedick loves her. (III, 1, 106-116)

To that one can add 39 instances of "see," and 10 of "sight." The eye motif demonstrates the caution with which one has to approach analyses of Shakespeare (and his contemporaries) confined to metaphors. The analyses of Spurgeon, Clemen, and others pass by the eye motif, because the word is normally a part of the literal text and not a metaphor at all.[7] The eye, an organ of perception, is in the dialectic of *A Midsummer Night's Dream* opposed to judgment. This opposition, which propels the major action, is early stated:

Hermia: I would my father looked but with my eyes.
Theseus: Rather your eyes must with his judgment look.
(I, 1, 56-57)

Naturally, Hermia revolts against this imposition: "O hell! to choose love by another's eye." (I, 1, 140) Yet Lysander's intuitive response seems almost to undercut the lovers' position:

Or, if there were a sympathy in choice,
War, death, or sickness did lay siege to it,
Making it momentany as a sound,
Swift as a shadow, short as any dream.
(I, 1, 141-144)

---

[7] This in no way, naturally, invalidates the points that criticism based on analysis of metaphor can legitimately make. And the play's images yield other matters of interest. Wolfgang Clemen, for instance (in *The Development of Shakespeare's Imagery*, London, 1951, pp. 94, 187), comments on the "earthiness" of *A Midsummer Night's Dream*, a quality stemming from the large number of plants and animals mentioned. This suggests that Shakespeare's techniques here are an anticipation of surrealism, that is, that in conveying the fantastic and unreal, it is necessary to concentrate closely upon fixing the objectively real.

"Shadow" and "dream" are the metaphoric associates of love, as even Lysander apprehends. "So quick bright things come to confusion," he states gloomily. (149) It reads almost like a male rationale for inconstancy, an underlying recognition that love will need an exit line. The female psychology is shown to be opposed to this, for Helena affirms: "Love looks not with the eyes, but with the mind." (i, 1, 234)

The women, at least, can say this, for Helena and Hermia do not deviate in their choice. The men, on the other hand, make lofty appeals to reason to justify their inconstancy. Lysander has a nicely ironic justification for his volte-face:

> The will of man is by his reason swayed,
> And reason says you are the worthier maid. . . .
> Reason becomes the marshal to my will,
> And leads me to your eyes, . . .
> (ii, 2, 115-116, 120-121)

So, under cover of "reason," comes the irrational rejection of Hermia. (ii, 2, 135-144) Demetrius, for his part, awakening to the sight of Helena, first breaks into an anthology of late-Petrarchan conceits (iii, 2, 137-144), then remembers to justify his spasm of adoration in these terms:

> Lysander, keep thy Hermia: I will none.
> If e'er I loved her, all that love is gone.
> My heart with her but as guestwise sojourned,
> And now to Helen is it home returned,
> There to remain.
> (iii, 2, 169-173)

97

The men, in brief, are subjectivists who advance their retinal impressions as objective and rational justifications for their conduct. "How," wonders Lysander, "can these things in me seem scorn to you,/Bearing the badge of faith to prove them true?" (III, 2, 126-127) "Faith": the eternal justification, through the ages, of the Romantic, the heretic, and the adolescent caught out in malfeasance. Helena is plainly no intellectual, but she, bred in the Shakespearean school of man-deflaters, deftly refutes Lysander's claims to "judgment":

Lysander: I had no judgment when to her I swore.
Helena: Nor none, in my mind, now you give her o'er.
                                              (III, 2, 134-135)

The female position, as in *Love's Labour's Lost*, is that the caprice of the eye must be subject to a primary discipline: the keeping of oaths.

That is as far as Shakespeare, in this play, cares to take his analysis of the aberrations of love. The affair is stabilized by Puck's application of the antidote, which—like the original love-juice—is directed toward the eye:

Puck: I'll apply
        To your eye,
        Gentle lover, remedy.
        When thou wak'st,
        Thou tak'st
        True delight
        In the sight
        Of thy former lady's eye;
                                              (III, 2, 450-457)

Object and subject, literal and symbolic come together in a single term: the eye. But following this central corrective to the lovers' vision comes the aftermath. The "awakening" sequence, perhaps the most poignant moment of poetry in the play, is in theatrical terms presented as a return to daylight and sanity.[8] The lovers speak with the accent of sincerity, and must play it with conviction. Yet, however feelingly Demetrius protests his conversion (IV, 1, 163-175), it is basically no more than a re-statement of his earlier passion for Hermia: "The object and the pleasure of mine eye/Is only Helena." (IV, 1, 169-170) The basic joke is that the male lovers' behavior is precisely the same, after as before the love-juice. Only the objects of their unique passions have changed. Even the metaphoric justifications remain unaltered: "But, like a sickness, did I loathe this food" (IV, 1, 172) says Demetrius of Hermia; earlier, his rejection of Helena included "For I am sick when I do look on you." (II, 1, 212) Lysander, being left in possession of the original status quo, has no need to explain his aberrant attachment to Helena, and says nothing about the matter. So the burden of reacting to, if not explaining the affair, passes to the women:

Hermia: Methinks I see these things with parted eye,
             When everything seems double.
Helena: So methinks;
             And I have found Demetrius, like a jewel,
             Mine own, and not mine own.

[8] Ernest Schanzer, "*A Midsummer Night's Dream*," *University of Toronto Quarterly*, XXIV (1955), 234.

Demetrius: Are you sure
          That we are awake? It seems to me
          That yet we sleep, we dream. Do not you
             think
          The duke was here, and bid us follow him?
Hermia: Yea, and my father.
Helena: And Hippolyta.
Lysander: And he did bid us follow to the temple.
Demetrius: Why then, we are awake. Let's follow him,
          And by the way let us recount our dreams.

                               Exeunt
                        (IV, 1, 188-198)

Even here, the sexual distinctions are marvelously preserved. The men question merely whether they sleep or
wake. They go off happy that they have awakened; all is
well. The women, more subtly, question the veracity of
their waking eye, and a tinge of doubt, of foreboding,
lingers in the wake of their departure. "Mine own, and
not mine" are virtually Helena's last words in the play.[9]

And so the four lovers pass from the center of the
stage, their relationships left on this poised, ambivalent
cadence. Their unquestioning faith in the absolute validity of their own subjectivism has, perhaps, been shaken
by the events of the night. For us, standing outside the
patterned movements of the quartet, the affair requires
a certain ironic detachment. The "dream" is Shakespeare's chosen analogy for the activity that provides the
major element in the play's action. One could call it

---

[9] It is worth noting that Hermia's dream (the only dream, in
the normal sense, reported in the play) contains a spasm of apprehension. (II, 2, 145-150)

Shakespeare's Allegory of Love. The best epigraph, perhaps, is H. L. Mencken's. "Love: the illusion that one woman is any different from another." It is an illusion that the author of *A Midsummer Night's Dream*, on the evidence, must have felt especially qualified to analyze, to dramatize, and to question.

III

From "dream," to "play": the minor action presents another species of illusion. The Bottom scenes amount to a commanding demonstration of Shakespeare's comic methods. Very broadly, one can say three things of these scenes. First, they are funny in themselves; second, they parody the principals, and their behavior, in the major action; third, they enable a matter of some intellectual substance to be analyzed. It is the third of these aspects that immediately concerns us, for on the first I have nothing to say, and the second can conveniently be deferred to a discussion of the relations between the major and minor actions. But the intellectual substance of the Bottom scenes, a critique of the mechanics of illusion, is worth pausing over.

The play scenes embody in themselves a set of illusionist variations. They exhibit the dramatic equivalent of a set of mutually reflecting mirrors; for, as M. C. Bradbrook remarks, "the fun puts both players and audience together inside the jest of professional actors pretending to be mechanicals trying to be amateur actors before an unreal audience."[10] The terminus of this

[10] M. C. Bradbrook, *Shakespeare and Elizabethan Poetry* (London, 1951), p. 157.

baroque speciality—it is an international jeu d'esprit—
one can see at the Prado, in the special room, complete
with mirror, which the Spanish authorities have provided
for the proper appreciation of Velasquez' "Los Meniñas."
This playing with reality is a part of the elegant mastery
which Shakespeare displays over the intellectual implications of his subject matter. It is, technically, another
stage in the dialogue between objective and subjective
which the play as a whole elaborates. However, the play
scenes do more than embody a refined dramatic jest, they
present a reasoned argument concerning the nature of
dramatic illusion. To Bottom fall the views that dramatist in the later seventeenth century would have refuted
in his prefaces or savaged in a pamphlet; it is merely
another way of making the same points. Indeed, the Bottom scenes have a latent ring of neoclassic criticism that
becomes almost explicit in the final scene, the courtiers
taking a notably didactic line. Essentially these establish, through criticism which is transcendentally inept,
the mechanics of illusion.

Bottom establishes himself first (i, 2) and his mental
dominance over his fellows; this is necessary for him to
get his own way in the sequel, the praxis of the theory.
In this scene his technical fatuities are confined to a
yearning to play as many parts as possible. (At which,
surely, a number of actors since must have murmured
"touché.") And Bottom connects the concerns of the
mechanicals with the larger affair of the play, through
its most persistent image: "If I do it, let the audience
look to its eyes." (i, 2, 22)

The central analysis of induced illusion is contained in

III, 1. Bottom, in his role of dramatic theorist, recommends:

(i) A prologue (Chorus) who does not merely make factual statements about the action to come, but reassures the audience of the insubstantiality of the pageant.

> Write me a prologue, and let the prologue seem to say, we will do no harm with our swords, and that Pyramus is not killed indeed; . . . This will put them out of fear.   (III, 1, 15-20)

(ii) A similar statement by the Lion, allied to the exposure of his face through the lion's mane:

> "I am a man as other men are." And there, indeed, let him name his name and tell them plainly he is Snug the joiner.   (III, 1, 39-40)

(iii) An approach to propertied spectacle which consists of capturing the literal implications of the dramatic fiction:

> Why, then may you leave a casement of the great chamber window, where we play, open, and the moon may shine in at the casement.   (III, 1, 48-50)

(iv) An actor, as Wall, to represent a nonanimate object.

All this appears to be palpable nonsense, and is certainly ludicrous in the sequel. Yet Bottom's recommendations have, in modified form, been advocated by considerably more reputable thinkers. (i) and (ii) amount to an advocacy of the *Verfremdungseffekt*, that is, a de-

103

struction by the players of the illusion that the play is a play. Reverse Bottom's aim ("this will put them out of fear") and we have the precise objective of Brecht and his late-morality followers, which is to assert that the social ills depicted in the play really do exist and should cause disquiet. It is a view that has led to some remarkable actor-audience confrontations; in 1969, the audiences in the Living Theatre, in London, were virtually manhandled by the actors in their didactic determination to put the audience into fear. On the evidence of *A Midsummer Night's Dream* especially, we must assume that Shakespeare repudiates this view, as being totally unsuited to the psychological requirements of serious drama. Low comedy is one thing; comedians have always sought a very direct relationship with their audience, and there is no doubt that Launce's part is written in the expectation that the player will commune directly with his public. But the presentation of tragedy—which is the aim of Bottom—or of serious drama, founders if the integrity of the play-illusion is not preserved. Strictly, the alternative is not drama at all, but a species of buffoonery or of popular sermon; which is precisely what, in Shakespeare's day, the drama had succeeded in climbing out of.

Again, (iii) has had a continuing vogue, then and now. Shakespeare may well have been deriding a view that had a certain currency in his day. The theater then relied (as Henslowe's diary makes clear) a great deal more on properties as aids to the imagination than panegyrists of the classic bareness of the Elizabethan dramatic tradition would have us believe. It was, after all, the way that the theater developed in the later seventeenth century; the spectacular is merely a species of the literal. And amazingly (as C. L. Barber reminds us) this same literalism was industriously celebrated in Reinhardt's film of *A Midsummer Night's Dream*. Shakespeare's view is that the imagination needs subtler stimuli than mere objective representations.[11]

The interlude, then, is not only "an essay on the art of destroying a play,"[12] it is an affirmation of the correct principles to which a dramatist should adhere. The endeavors of the mechanicals stimulate some competent, if obvious, dramatic criticism by the courtiers. It hardly calls for detailed comment, but one detects the note of neoclassic exposition of rule-breaking. "This is the greatest error of all the rest" exclaims the judicious Theseus (v, 1, 240); and Demetrius is loudest as the voice of reason. "Why, all these should be in the lanthorn, for all these are in the moon" (v, 1, 254-255) he crows, responding to Starveling's dogged catalogue of correspondences. The underlying joke here is that Demetrius, adopting rather too heartily the approach that anticipates John Dennis', is by decree of Oberon left permanently and irretrievably in a state of illusion. "Error" was Oberon's word. It leaves a tart aftertaste of a comment on Demetrius, that notable judge of reality and illusion. In all, then, the interlude and its reactions constitute the thematic complement in the main enquiry of the play: how reality is to be assessed, how the evidence of one's

[11] The point is familiar to television producers, who find that televised poetry readings, for example, are singularly ill-adapted to explicit visual images that directly embody the text.

[12] Righter, *op.cit.*, p. 108.

eyes is to be judged. They compose a structural antithesis to the lovers' scenes which can be stated thus: the lovers declare illusion to be reality; the actors declare reality to be illusion.

IV

The "play" and "dream" symbols have a certain natural affinity. But their relationship is also a subtly hostile one. In a Shakespearean romantic comedy, romance commonly comes under several sorts of fire. It is the function of the minor action in *A Midsummer Night's Dream* to criticize the major. This implicit criticism (which supports the explicit criticisms of Theseus and Puck) consists in the first case of the affinity between "play" and "dream," for both point to a state of induced illusion. The matter is, however, elaborated beyond the nuances of implicit comparison.

The play scenes very obviously parody the affairs of Demetrius and Helena, Lysander and Hermia. It is a parallelism of subject matter: love, a serious business to the quartet, is burlesqued by Pyramus and Thisbe. We need only note that *intent* to satirize is not at all an essential with Shakespeare's comedians. Some (Speed, Feste) do; some (Bottom, Dogberry) do not. It does not matter; Shakespeare supplies the intention in all instances, whether or not his clowns have the brains to be aware of the importance of their function. The general parody of love is, of course, uniquely concentrated on the metamorphosis of Bottom. Apart from his dramatic labors, his penetration into the fairy world extends the dimensions of his parodic existence. His ass's head, "unaware-ness concretized,"[13] embodies like the love-juice a symbolic reality; it is a further element in the allegory of love. The Titania-Bottom relationship is, indeed, a reductio ad absurdum of love.[14] (For that matter, Bottom the Tyrant—IV, 1—is a lampoon on the Duke. Everyone in this play, it seems, must take some knocks.) Yet in this situation, enticed by the doting Titania, Bottom finds the words—it is a fine stroke—to make an overt, and perfectly intelligent comment on love: "And yet, to say the truth, reason and love keep little company together nowadays." (III, 1, 130-131) This is clear enough, but less obviously central is the point Bottom goes on to make: "The more the pity that some honest neighbors will not make them friends." (III, 1, 131-132) This, surely, supports Theseus' persuasions at the start of the play. Some benevolent advice, from one knowing both parties, does not come amiss in matters of love. It is one of the bedrock comments set into the play, validated by Bottom's status as "wise" (in effect) fool.

One can, in fact, overdo the "multiple viewpoint" approach to a Shakespearean play. Theseus, Puck, and Bottom all say virtually the same thing about love. They hold the strongest action-defining views expressed in *A Midsummer Night's Dream*. Theseus' advice to the lovers, Bottom's fund of proverbial wisdom, and Puck's cynical "Lord, what fools these mortals be!" (III, 2, 115) all substantiate the view of love implicit in the play-idea.

[13] Bertrand Evans, *Shakespeare's Comedies* (Oxford, 1960), p. 44.
[14] Schanzer, *op.cit.*, p. 234.

But satire is not all. The two symbols seem to converge, rather than continue their latent antipathy, in the final scenes. The dialogue between subjective and objective is to achieve a kind of resolution after all, "the concord of this discord." Theseus and Hippolyta debate it, in the exchange that sounds the note of reconciliation that pervades the close. His skeptical account of the lunatic, the lover, and the poet (this must mean "dramatist" here) concedes the power of the imagination to create internally convincing shapes, but denies them any objective existence. (v, 1, 2-22) Yet Hippolyta, for all her scornful common sense, suggests thoughtfully that the imagination creates its own structures, which have their own kind of validity:

> But all the story of the night told over,
> And all their minds transfigured so together,
> More witnesseth than fancy's images
> And grows to something of great constancy;
> But howsoever, strange and admirable.
>
> (v, 1, 23-27)

This miniature debate is extended during the interlude, with the debating roles reversed. Hippolyta can find no virtue in the antics of the players, while Theseus, largely out of his princely courtesy, defends the activities of the illusionists:

Hippolyta: This is the silliest stuff that ever I heard.
Theseus: The best in this kind are but shadows; and the worst are no worse, if imagination amend them.

Hippolyta: It must be your imagination then, and not theirs.

Theseus: If we imagine no worse of them than they of themselves, they may pass for excellent men.

(v, 1, 208-214)

In the immediate context, Theseus is deftly winning an argument by turning Hippolyta's own words against her. But the words gather to themselves an easy, symbolic weight. "Shadows" brings all together; it means actors, but it merges with night and dreams. It touches, perhaps, the softly-iterated "nothings" that measure the final scene:

Philostrate: And it is nothing, nothing in the world; . . .

(v, 1, 78)

Hippolyta: He says they can do nothing in this kind.

Theseus: The kinder we, to give them thanks for nothing.

(v, 1, 88-89)

Lysander: He is nothing.   (v, 1, 301)

It signifies the bell that later tolls for the "insubstantial pageant ended"; the contention between illusion and reality, objective and subjective, all closes upon "a kind of nothing." The two symbols embrace at the last, for "shadow" and "dream," brought together by Puck, have their own centripetal tendencies:

If we shadows have offended,
Think but this, and all is mended—
That you have but slumb'red here

109

While these visions did appear.
And this weak and idle theme,
No more yielding but a dream, . . .

(v, 1, 412-417)

Night becomes a context, not for illusion, but repose and harmony. The poised ending suggests the only possible resolution to the antitheses of the play. And with Puck, the theme of reconciliation becomes overt at the last: "Give me your hands, if we be friends,/And Robin shall restore amends."

CHAPTER VI

The Merchant of Venice

Of few Shakespeare plays, I suppose, does our experience vary so widely as with *The Merchant of Venice*. We come to it, at school, as a simple melodrama. We may retain this interpretation into adult life, intellectualized as allegory. Justice versus mercy is a respectable codification of the issues generated in the trial scene.[1] Or we can view the play as a potentially subversive study of human relationships mediated by money. It is a difficult play.[2] Though it is not normally discussed in the context of *All's Well That Ends Well* and *Measure for Measure* (its dating is secure to about 1596), *The Merchant of Venice* seems to belong to the world of the problem comedies.

---

[1] This line is developed by Nevill Coghill, in "The Governing Idea: Essays in the Interpretation of Shakespeare," *Shakespeare Quarterly I* (1948).

[2] In recent years, assessments have ranged between two poles represented by Frank Kermode and A. D. Moody: "It [*The Merchant of Venice*] begins with usury and corrupt love; it ends with harmony and perfect love." Frank Kermode, "The Mature Comedies," in *Early Shakespeare*, ed. J. R. Brown and Bernard Harris (London, 1961), p. 224.

The opposite judgment stresses the central irony of *The Merchant of Venice*: ". . . the play does not celebrate the Christian virtues so much as expose their absence." A. D. Moody, *Shakespeare: The Merchant of Venice* (London, 1964), p. 10.

The problems start with the title. Shakespeare normally identifies the play's protagonist by name in his title. To identify by category may pose a covert question. What sort of "Gentlemen" are *The Two Gentlemen of Verona*? Who is the real "Shrew" in *The Taming of the Shrew*—Katherina or Bianca? Here, one asks: who is the "Merchant"? Surely, Antonio: the cast list makes it clear that Antonio is "a Merchant of *Venice*," and Shylock "the rich Jew." But it is reasonable to regard Shylock as a merchant of sorts. The parallelism, and latent confrontation of the two is evident throughout the play.[3] And Portia enters the Court of Justice with the striking question: "Which is the merchant here? and which the Jew?" (IV, 1, 172)[4] Thus the trial presents a dramatic ikon that expresses the latent question of the title: who is the merchant of Venice? And what sort of person is he?

Our experience of the title, I suggest, is analogous to our experience of the play. The "obvious" reading fails

[3] This view of the play's construction is very convincingly elaborated by Graham Midgley, in "*The Merchant of Venice*: A Reconsideration," *Essays in Criticism*, x (1960).

[4] H. C. Goddard has written illuminatingly on the import of this line. He also emphasizes the significance of the play's original title. (It was entered in the Stationers' Register (1598) as *The Marchaunt of Venyce or otherwise called the Jewe of Venyce*.) See H. C. Goddard, *The Meaning of Shakespeare* (Chicago, 1951). Its symbolic implications aside, Portia's question suggests that Antonio and Shylock are not dissimilarly dressed. "Jewish gaberdine" notwithstanding (gaberdine is a material, and not a style), the visual distinction between Antonio and Shylock cannot be so apparent as to make the question superfluous. In Jonathan Miller's production for the National Theatre (London, 1970) Antonio and Shylock were both dressed as (nineteenth century) businessmen.

to still our questions. In the theater, we may participate readily in the excitements of the trial, and respond to the almost unflawed lyricism of the final Act. But afterwards: commentator after commentator has written of the unease that the play leaves with him. The alien Shylock and the alienated Antonio; the patness, almost glibness, of the accord between Portia and Nerissa, and their forsworn men, so different from the conclusion of *Love's Labour's Lost*; Jessica, who has done so well out of robbing her father, whispering with Lorenzo of Cressida, of Dido, of Medea. . . . These are shadows over the moon of Belmont. I think that we must plainly recognize that ambivalence is central to our experience of *The Merchant of Venice*. I do not seek to explain away this ambivalence, to find a solution that smoothes away the difficulties. What I propose to do is to investigate, and try to define, some of the areas of difficulty in this play.

I

The most inviting approach to *The Merchant of Venice* lies, I suggest, through its linguistic texture. It is clear that the play's linguistic identity, as it were, is manifest not so much in images as in a small group of associated words of mainly literal status. The key word I take to be "venture"; and it is obviously linked with "hazard," "thrift," "usury," "fortune," "lottery," and "advantage." These terms recur steadily throughout the play. What they have in common is the idea of *gain*, with a varying degree of risk attached. Suppose, then, that we conceive of the play as a conjugation of the verb *to gain*. All the relationships in the play (with, I think, the sole exception of Old Gobbo and Launcelot) dramatize this verb. The nominal activity of the dramatis personae is in considerable part, love. What the play demonstrates is the interconnections of love and money. So the terms I have cited extend from commerce to personal relations. The formal principle of *The Merchant of Venice*, then, I take to be a series of mutations of "venture."

"Venture" virtually opens the play. As a noun, it means a commercial enterprise involving some risk; and its specific application is to overseas trading. It is in this sense that "venture" is introduced, forming the staple of the conversation of Antonio and his friends. Thus the word is fixed to Antonio's trading operations, and to the literal world of commerce. (I, 1, 15, 21, 42) But the associated words refuse to be so fixed. Portia, employing "venture" as a verb, associates it with "hazard" in her dialogue with Bassanio: "Before you hazard, . . ./ Before you venture for me." (III, 2, 2 . . . 10) The context is love, and the meaning of "venture" here is simply "risk." Again, "thrift" is essentially a commercial term, meaning "profit"; it is in this sense that Antonio and Shylock debate its application in I, 3. The word is however employed in the more general sense of "success," especially in love. Thus Bassanio: "I have a mind presages me such thrift/That I should questionless be fortunate!" (I, 1, 175-176) And Morocco: "Thrive I as I may . . ." (II, 7, 60) Bassanio does a little more to erode the firm, literal status of "venture." Elaborating his "arrow" metaphor, he introduces the verb "adventure": "and by adventuring both/I oft found both." (I, 1, 143-144) The word is thus linked with "hazard," in "Or bring your hazard back again" (I, 1, 151), and so to the casket scenes and the repeated motto: "Who chooseth me must give and hazard all he hath." The point I seek to establish is that "venture," in conjunction with its associated terms, has no really firm basis of meaning (as the play unfolds). It tends to slide away from the literal, commercial sense to the more generalized sense of personal gain; almost, indeed, to the overtly metaphoric. The drift of the play is to suggest that "venture," so firmly literal in the opening scene, is in fact a figure for human activity. The ambivalence that we detect as the central experience of the play applies to its core of language.

II

This argument is buttressed if we agree to regard "ships" (the nominal embodiment of "venture") as the symbolic extension of Antonio. There is a very broad hint that we should do so in the opening scene. Salerio introduces a crucial simile:

Your mind is tossing on the ocean,
There where your argosies with portly sail—
Like signiors and rich burghers on the flood, . . .

(I, 1, 8-10)

This is a clear enough instance of the associative, i.e., metaphor-making mind in action. State the trope, "A merchant is like a ship," and few will miss the point. State "A ship is like a merchant" and as few will hit it. Yet both statements are the same, not in logic, but in the realm of the imagination. One must certainly distinguish, technically, between symbol and metaphor so far as it is

115

possible.[5] Ships are a literal presence in the play, off stage, and thus gather to themselves a symbolic weight. They also furnish metaphors in a few passages, notably Gratiano's image. (II, 6, 14-19) My view is that symbol and metaphor tend to fuse in this play (as they do, for example, in the flower-humanity analogies of *The Winter's Tale*, IV, 4), and that the "ship" allusions form a collective figure, a running parallel to the situation of Antonio. When, therefore, Solanio says

> Believe me, sir, had I such venture forth,
> The better part of my affections would
> Be with my hopes abroad.
>
> (I, 1, 15-17)

we are to understand the true situation of the distrait Antonio. He, in plain terms, is the "wealthy Andrew," whose personal calamity is symbolically foreshadowed in the apprehensions of Salerio. But the parallelism of a ship and Antonio is not a blatant and restricted symbolic equation. The great masters of symbolism do not create thus. Sartre, discussing Tintoretto, makes the point:

> Tintoretto did not choose that yellow rift in the sky above Golgotha to *signify* anguish or to *provoke* it. It is anguish and yellow sky at the same time. Not sky of anguish or anguished sky; it is an anguish become thing, an anguish which has turned into yellow rift of sky, and which thereby is submerged and impasted by the proper qualities of things, by their

[5] A distinction is attempted in Ralph Berry, "The Frontier of Metaphor and Symbol," in *The British Journal of Aesthetics*, VII (1967), 76-83.

impermeability, their extension, their blind perma-
nence, their externality, and that infinity of relations
which they maintain with other things. That is, it is
no longer *readable*.[6]

Similarly, the ship *is* Antonio, and his hopes, disaster,
and salvation. The parallels, which are scattered through-
out the play, are too obvious to warrant discussion here.
I should add, however, that I find entirely convincing
N. Nathan's speculation that Shakespeare knew that
"Goodwins" meant "good friends":[7]

Salerio: Why, yet it lives there unchecked that Antonio
hath a ship of rich lading wracked on the nar-
row seas—the Goodwins I think they call the
place, a very dangerous flat, and fatal, where
the carcasses of many a tall ship lie buried as
they say, if my gossip Report be an honest
woman of her word.
                                                            (III, 1, 2-7)

So Antonio is wrecked on the shoals of friendship. The
alternative to Nathan's suggestion is a happy accident of,
to me, a high degree of improbability. And the play ends,
for Antonio, on this cadence:

Sweet lady, you have given me life and living!
For here I read for certain that my ships
Are safely come to road.
                                                    (v, 1, 286-288)

[6] J.-P. Sartre, *What Is Literature?* trans. Bernard Frechtman
(New York, 1965), p. 3.

[7] N. Nathan, *Names*, VII (1959), p. 191. Cited by J. R. Brown
in the New Arden edition of *The Merchant of Venice* (London,
1964), p. 70.

III

I now return to "venture." First, I want to examine
the implications of "venture" (in its literal sense of "commercial enterprise") that are touched on, if not properly
investigated, in the confrontation between Antonio and
Shylock in I, 3. All arguments, it is said, are arguments
about words. So it is here. There are two words that
Antonio and Shylock apply respectively to their professional activities: "Venture" and "thrift." These are both
hurrah-words. (Bassanio even applies "thrift" to his project of marrying Portia, I, 1, 175.) In the clash between
Antonio and Shylock, "venture" and "thrift" are opposed
to "usury" and "interest." These are boo-words, and Shylock's muttered "my well-won thrift,/Which he calls interest" establishes the antithesis. (I, 3, 46-47) The real
question, naturally, is how far these emotive labels describe the same process.

The opposition is between "venture" and "interest."
"Venture" applies to overseas trading with an apparent
element of risk attached. "Interest" is a fairly safe means
of ensuring steady profits, at home. At first sight, the two
modes of profit-making are quite different. That is the
line that Antonio takes. He holds to it stoutly when Shylock probes him:

Methoughts you said you neither lend nor borrow
Upon advantage.
                    I do never use it.

affirms Antonio. (I, 3, 65-66) Shylock then proceeds to
the spun-out tale of Jacob's dealings with his Uncle

118

Laban's sheep. (It is curious that this passage is often cut in performance: the metaphoric association of money-making and breeding is intellectually at the center of the play.) He concludes with "This was a way to thrive, and he was blest;/And thrift is blessing if men steal it not." (I, 3, 85-86) The implicit question is: isn't this a legitimate (if sharp) means of profit-making? But Antonio will have none of Shylock's attempt to annex his (intellectual, and thus moral) territory.

> This was a *venture*, sir, that Jacob served for,
> A thing not in his power to bring to pass,
> But swayed and fashioned by the hand of heaven.
> Was this inserted to make interest good?
> Or is your gold and silver ewes and rams?
>
> (I, 3, 87-91)

This is clear enough. A "venture" is morally defensible because it has an uncertain outcome, i.e., requires the decision of Heaven; it is, as we should say, something of a gamble. Whereas interest-taking, apparently, is stigmatized by the relative certainty of its profits.

But the matter isn't as simple as that. Antonio's position, that a "venture" is respectable because of the risk attached, is extremely feeble. Moral distinctions are not established by gradation of risk. Antonio's line sounds oddly reminiscent of the tendency, which J. K. Galbraith noted, for the chairmen of vast corporations, each possessing more stability than half the members of the United Nations, to laud the virtues of enterprise and competition, i.e., risk. The aim of commerce, in the past no less than now, has always been to reduce if possible to

zero the uncertainties attendant upon making money.
But we ought to examine Antonio's claim in the light
of the associations an Elizabethan would bring to it.
For him, "venture" would connote the spectacular State/
private-enterprise syndicates of the late sixteenth century: the voyages, part-war, part-exploration, part-trade
of Raleigh, Frobisher, Fenton, and many others. This
form of investment enjoyed the highest repute. The
Queen backed such voyages; the Court backed them; the
great city magnates backed them. The risks were admit-
tedly substantial. But if only one ship in three returned
home, the investor might show a sound profit. If the
enterprise were lucky, a number of fortunes would be
made. Fortunes could be lost, certainly—though not by
any one man, unless he were exceptionally rash—and
nothing afterwards matched the profits of Drake's voy-
age of 1577-1580, which yielded a return of £47 on
every pound invested. That, however, was only the most
spectacular of the ventures. Far less ambitious alternatives existed. By 1596, the merchants of Bristol had for
years been making very considerable, steady profits from
the imports of luxury goods from the Indies—spice,
hides, sugar. To stress the element of "risk" in that context—a context of which the *Merchant*'s original audience would be fully aware—would be rather naive.
Furthermore, the element of risk would be minimized by
spreading one's investment over a number of ventures:
this is the principle Antonio alludes to in "My ventures
are not in one bottom trusted." (I, 1, 42) Given normal
ventures in Tripoli, Mexico, England, Lisbon, Barbary,
and India (III, 2, 268-269), one would have to be quite

astonishingly unlucky to lose the lot. This is what happens to Antonio in Act III; quite. But it is hardly a convincing way of winning an argument in Act I.

IV

So Antonio, who had stressed the element of *safety* while discussing his ventures with Salerio and Solanio, stresses the element of *risk* with Shylock. It is not a position distinguished for intellectual consistency, or conviction. And underlying the literal, or manifest meaning is the metaphoric. This undercurrent of debate is obliquely hinted at by Shylock, and perhaps understood by Antonio.

The prevailing custom, in the Venice of the play as in England, was that money was lent gratis to friends and with interest to strangers. That is a way of putting it. Another is to say that by lending out money gratis, one makes the recipient one's friend. It was, no doubt, a congenial way of cementing amity between the high-born and those, however cultivated, in trade. Shylock does not speculate overtly on Antonio's motives, but he records the fact: "He lends out money gratis and brings down/ The rate of usance here with us in Venice." (I, 3, 40-41) And Antonio's opening words to Shylock confirm this: it is a claim to moral superiority too strident to be called effortless:

> Shylock, albeit I neither lend nor borrow
> By taking nor by giving of excess,
> Yet to supply the ripe wants of my friend,
> I'll break a custom. (I, 3, 57-60)

121

A velleity of language is worth noting here. Is there not the merest trace of emphasis in "*my* friend"? Would not "*a* friend" be, fractionally, the expected usage? Granted, that would create a possibly undesired collocation, "a friend . . . a custom." But would not "*a* friend . . . *my* custom" be the natural way of ordering the phrase? These things are slight, but a gossamer can show the way the wind blows. One is entitled to speculate on the basis of the friendship between Antonio and his "most noble kinsman," Bassanio. (i, 1, 57) The answer need involve no excess of cynicism. Still, a habit of pressing interest free loans on one's friends does nothing to diminish the attraction of even the most civilized and charming of men. When, therefore, Antonio interrupts Shylock's tale of Jacob, he exposes himself to a killing riposte:

Antonio: And what of him? Did he take interest?
Shylock: No, not take interest—not as you would say
Directly int'rest.

(i, 3, 71-73)

"*Directly* int'rest": that is the play, in two words. Shylock, the voice of reality in this play, states obliquely but unmistakably that there is no such thing as an interest free loan.

But if this is so, what is left of Antonio's position? Antonio is an intelligent man. He is compelled, by a freak of circumstances, to argue with a man whom he loathes and despises. He has to find one solid, intellectually valid reason to endorse the propositions: I am better than you, I am different from you. And he can find nothing better than the claim that ventures are "swayed and fashioned by the hand of heaven." Yet some ventures are, overall, virtual certainties; and for that matter difficulties may arise in gathering in one's interest on a loan. What, then, is left? Only a weak gibe, "or is your gold and silver ewes and rams?" The short answer is: yes. Shylock fashions his answer more elegantly: "I cannot tell; I make it breed as fast." And that pregnant phrase in effect concludes the debate. For the impersonal will of money is to breed; and Antonio has failed to demonstrate the moral superiority of his breeding methods. Moreover, he fails to take up the covert charge that there are more ways than one of accepting interest. The intellectual weakness becomes the psychological weakness, vis-à-vis Shylock. Hence Antonio, called upon to refute the Jew, can only reject him: "The devil can cite Scripture for his purpose." (i, 3, 94) That is abuse, not argument. The fact is that Shylock has refuted Antonio's claims to moral superiority; and Antonio, I think, knows it.

Hence Antonio—disturbed, shaken, somehow aware of the weaknesses in his position—is in no condition to penetrate Shylock's design. Rather, he blunders forward into the trap. The bond is dangerous as well as ludicrous; yet Antonio cannot retreat without loss of face. For Antonio's own arguments and attitudes bind him to that position. He wants the money; he will not borrow at high interest, "giving of excess"; he must accept at face value Shylock's wish for friendship, dramatized in a spectacularly frivolous bond; to reject the Jew's proposal is to show signs of fear, to rate such a creature as capable of danger; he wishes, perhaps, to make an imposing gesture before his friend, Bassanio. It is a complex of motives, and we have not exhausted them.

V

We can now attack directly the central problem of Antonio's psychology. The melancholy that shrouds him is surely neurotic in origin. Certainly the events presented in the play, and especially the issues discussed in the foregoing pages, contribute to this melancholy. The sense of weakness, of having been *refuted* as a man, is in my judgment a part of the situation of passivity and defeat that Antonio reveals in the trial scene. But there is more yet to sift. Using profits from overseas speculations to subsidize friends does not, in itself, account for Antonio's malaise, which in any case opens the play. What sort of man is Antonio, and why does he do the things he does? More specifically: can we identify the neurosis that appears to grip him?

On the evidence of I, 3, Antonio's conduct is characterized by a sense that the other caricatures one's self. It is very important to Antonio that he should be un-Jewish, that no possible parallel should exist between his and Shylock's vocations. Hence he overcompensates, insists on distinctions that he dare not pursue, and is much ruder to Shylock than Bassanio (who is socially superior to them both). For it is above all necessary for Antonio to stand well with Bassanio. His whole pattern of conduct toward Bassanio, flamboyantly generous throughout, hints at a secret terror lest any should perceive the remotest resemblance between *his* relationships and a

Jew's. For that might impair his understanding with Bassanio.

And here we have to reflect on another aspect of Antonio's relationship with Bassanio. The *fact*, presented by the play, is that Antonio's emotional life is fixed upon Bassanio. That is all. Yet critics have been ready to argue that the secret of Antonio's depression is his repressed homosexual desire for Bassanio.[8] The term "homosexual," nevertheless, limits, prejudges, and distorts the situation. One is immediately condemned to a labored parade of the term's implications: that some degree of homosexuality is present in all, that thwarted homosexuality (if present) is not necessarily the key to Antonio's melancholy, even that Renaissance conventions made extravagant male friendships fashionable, and so on. It hardly seems worth while to elaborate the unprovable. Sartre again seems relevant here: a homosexual, he has remarked, is a man who practices homosexuality. Anyone who does not, is entitled to the dignity of his choice. My own view is that Antonio's behavior is consistent with a repressed homosexual desire for Bassanio, and that the actor may perfectly well interpret the part along these lines. But we ought not to attach the label "homosexual" as though it mastered and explained the situation.

What, then, is my explanation for the conduct of Antonio? I return to the key word, "venture." That word has several near-synonyms in *The Merchant of Venice*. None of them is the simple word we should use, in mod-

[8] See, for example, Midgley, *op.cit.*; and John Wain, *The Living World of Shakespeare* (Harmondsworth, England, 1964).

ern English, to express the essential psychological quality of the action. That word is *gamble*.

No one, so far as I know, has concentrated on the
implications of *gamble* in the context of this play, though
critics often use the term in passing to describe Antonio's
reckless acceptance of the bond. Yet gambling is a pro-
foundly significant human activity, which today possesses
an extensive literature on its operations and psychology.
The classic work on the subject is Edmund Bergler's *The
Psychology of Gambling*,[9] which I now draw upon to
substantiate my view of Antonio.

Many people indulge in a mild, occasional gamble.
But Bergler's study is concerned with neurotic gambling.
His central thesis is that the neurotic gambler plays to
lose. "The unconscious wish to lose becomes . . . an in-
tegral part of the gambler's inner motivations." (p. 24)
The mechanism of this compulsion to lose he analyzes
into three stages:

(i) "Unconscious provocation of a situation in which
they are rejected and defeated."

(ii) "Attack, full of hatred and seemingly in self-
defense, aimed at their self-constructed enemies."

(iii) "Self-pity, and the enjoyment of unconscious
psychic masochistic pleasure." (p. 31)

Psychic masochism, "denotes the unconscious craving for
defeat, humiliation, rejection, pain." (p. 24) It constitutes the consummation of the process, and the objective
of the gambler.

[9] Edmund Bergler, *The Psychology of Gambling* (New York,
1958).

126

Now this, which is a generalized structure of the gambler's psychology, fits Antonio very well. Indeed, one could argue that the play's opening line, "In sooth I know not why I am so sad" reveals not so much depression as that ennui which, we are told, is the classic state of the gambler before a hazard. But let us consider the three phases of the mechanism.

(i) "Unconscious provocation of a situation . . ." Antonio's fortunes are extraordinarily extended, even in Act I. Salerio and Solanio both feel he *ought* to be worrying more about his ventures. Shylock, the auditor of the play's persons and values, states that "his means are in supposition." (I, 3, 16) Indeed they are. Of six ventures, four are outside the Mediterranean—Antonio's normal field of operations—and two, Mexico and India, are manifestly hazardous. There is no safe local trading here, no real insurance. Yet Antonio acts as a bottomless reservoir of funds for his friend; he is as extravagant a backer as Bassanio a spender. Over and above his ambitious trading ventures, Antonio pledges his person. He seems to court risks: perhaps out of a desire to hazard all for Bassanio, and by losing his principal—his body—gain a supremacy in Bassanio's affections. The motivation is not incompatible with my earlier suggestions. We have to read the sudden decision "Content, in faith. I'll seal to such a bond" (I, 3, 148) from our experience of life, in which such critical decisions are made by the mind for causes which the intellect cannot compass. Here I stress the darker side of the mind, the self-destructive urge which impels the gambler to place his all, not a part, at

127

hazard. Certainly Antonio has a responsibility for his difficulties, that does not square with his later adoption of the role of passive tool of fate.

(ii) The "attack, full of hatred . . . aimed at . . . self-constructed enemies" clearly applies to Antonio's relations with Shylock. What is marked about Antonio is the extraordinary virulence of his hatred of Shylock. Of course, all the Christians loathe him. Salerio and Solanio jeer at him, Launcelot leaves his service, Bassanio can scarcely contain his distaste for him. But at least the Venetians (prior to the trial scene) treat Shylock as an intensely unlikeable human being. Antonio treats him like a dog. "You spit on me on Wednesday last,/You spurned me such a day, another time/You called me dog." (I, 3, 122-124) Is there not something pathological in the intensity of hate which Antonio brings to his dealings with Shylock?

(iii) "Self-pity, and the enjoyment of unconscious psychic masochistic pleasure." This, I suggest, is consistent with Antonio's behavior following the bond agreement. There are two reported passages. First, Salerio describes the parting with Bassanio:

> I saw Bassanio and Antonio part:
> Bassanio told him he would make some speed
> Of his return; he answered, "Do not so.
> Slubber not business for my sake, Bassanio,
> But stay the very riping of the time;
> And for the Jew's bond which he hath of me,
> Let it not enter in your mind of love.
> Be merry, and employ your chiefest thoughts

To courtship and such fair ostents of love
As shall conveniently become you there."
And even there, his eye being big with tears,
Turning his face, he put his hand behind him,
And with affection wondrous sensible
He wrung Bassanio's hand; and so they parted.

(II, 8, 36-49)

Is there not here a somewhat feminine quality, a quality expressed commonly in the words: "Don't put yourself out on *my* account"? Antonio's is the unmistakable voice of the woman currently eclipsed by the more dashing rival, and determined to extract the utmost moral gratification from the situation. This is even more apparent in the letter Antonio sends Bassanio:

Sweet Bassanio, my ships have all miscarried, my creditors grow cruel, my estate is very low, my bond to the Jew is forfeit. And since in paying it, it is impossible I should live, all debts are cleared between you and I if I might but see you at my death. Notwithstanding, use your pleasure. If your love do not persuade you to come, let not my letter.

(III, 2, 315-321)

Even the syntax is feminine: the fluctuating "if . . . notwithstanding . . . if . . ." The "if your love do not persuade you to come, let not my letter" is especially revealing. It is almost coquettish. But it is also the voice of one thriving on rejection: really, is there any likelihood that Bassanio would *not* come?

What Antonio wants, in brief, is to suffer and to have

129

Bassanio witness it. He says as much. "Pray God Bassanio come/To see me pay his debt, and then I care not!" (III, 3, 35-36) The trial scene finds Antonio fully resigned to the extremity of his sentence: there is no life force left in the man.

> I do oppose
> My patience to his fury, and am armed
> To suffer with a quietness of spirit
> The very tyranny and rage of his.
>
> (IV, 1, 10-13)

Indeed, he positively urges the Court to proceed to judgment, on not less than three occasions (83, 116, 241-242). It all comes down to the extraordinarily interesting and revealing metaphor that Antonio chooses to express his situation: "I am a tainted wether of the flock,/Meetest for death." (IV, 1, 114-115) A wether, though scarcely any critic appears conscious of this simple fact, is a castrated ram. Wethers cannot breed. Hence, with a sad irony, Antonio refers back to his earlier exchange with Shylock:

Antonio: Or is your gold and silver ewes and rams?
Shylock: I cannot tell; I make it breed as fast.

> (I, 3, 91-92)

Antonio's financial operations have proven sterile. But surely the human implications of "wether" go beyond the allusion to trading methods. "Wether" offers a metaphoric comment on Antonio's situation that can accommodate the homosexual theory (if one wishes), or suggest something quite different. I do not pursue the speculation; but Antonio's sense of failure, his readiness—even longing—for death, are marked. Both as a man, and as merchant-venturer, Antonio is sterile. The metaphor dominates him.

So far, then, Antonio's conduct fits the generalized structure of the neurotic gambler. But we can do better than this. Bergler distinguishes several subcategories of gambler, one of which seems strikingly applicable to Antonio. It is the passive-feminine male gambler. Bergler describes the type thus: "This type displays the characteristics of the classical gambler, with the addition of a tendency toward unconscious feminine identification. This identification makes it possible for him to enjoy, in defeat, the emotional sensation of being overwhelmed." (p. 87) As I have already suggested, there is a certain feminine quality in Antonio. "Passive-feminine" appears an ideal way of characterizing him. And the "tendency toward unconscious feminine identification" is pronounced in Antonio's final "bid her be judge/Whether Bassanio had not once a love." (IV, 1, 274-275) It is interesting that Bergler, discussing this type, raises the obvious possibility only to reject it: "This type of neurotic is often unjustly accused of being a homosexual pervert. He is not a homosexual, and never becomes one. The structure of perversion homosexuality is quite different." (p. 87) If the passive-feminine gambler is not a homosexual, then, what sort of relationships does he tend to form? Here again Bergler has a suggestive answer:

Passive-feminine gamblers consistently seek "stronger" partners. The women they choose to marry are

131

THE MERCHANT OF VENICE

shrews; the men they choose for their friends are "strong," "superior" characters, who exploit or dominate them. Submissive, always on the lookout for someone to admire, they are the typical followers. They are of course unconscious of all this, since lack of initiative and absence of normal activity are easily rationalized.

(pp. 87-88)

This applies exactly to Antonio and Bassanio. Bassanio, of course, is really a fairly tough character. His suppliant situations in the play should not deceive us. He is extraordinarily good at getting his own way, and reveals a basic shrewdness in the crisis of the casket choice. Bassanio is the type of aristocrat who exploits his charm to ensure that he is never on the losing side. What he risks is other people's money. Bassanio is one of life's winners; no wonder Antonio admires him.

In sum, Antonio exhibits a recognizable (in twentieth century terms) neurosis,[10] that of the passive-feminine gambler; this is the key to his conduct and personal relations. His commercial activities are not merely a source of income; they express the cast of his mind. *Venture*, for him, is a high-risk activity whose ultimate psychological objective is a personal disaster allied to certain

[10] I am assuming that we can legitimately use the term here: that is, that Shakespeare has incorporated into his play a case history similar to those which later medical research has identified and categorized. But the nature of the neurosis is obviously debatable. Dr. W.I.D. Scott, in his medical study of morbid psychology in Shakespeare, regards Antonio as an endogenous depressive, that is, one whose depression arises from no ascertainable cause. See W.I.D. Scott, *Shakespeare's Melancholics* (London, 1962), pp. 35-46.

compensatory satisfactions. The pound of flesh that Shylock demands has its hidden counterpart in the price Antonio exacts of Bassanio: that he should come, "To see me pay his debt, and then I care not!"

VI

Shylock is Antonio's complement. If Antonio's symbolic extension is the ship, hazarding and vulnerable, Shylock's is the house, secure and guarded. "Look to my house. . . . But stop my house's ears—I mean my casements; . . . Do as I bid you; shut doors after you. . . ." (II, 5, 16 . . . 33 . . . 51) If Antonio's verb, his essential impulse, is "venture," Shylock's is "thrive." "Thrifty mind" is, it seems, the highest praise he can bestow. (II, 5, 53) It is perfectly in keeping with the man that he should lend money upon interest; his route to personal gain is close, slow, certain. Not for him the brilliant hazards of the overseas market. And his underlying satisfactions complement Antonio's. Antonio displays a humor of melancholy, Shylock of hate. "I'll not answer that,/ But say it is my humor." (IV, 1, 42-43) Antonio's advantage is in submission, Shylock's in killing. He will seize on Antonio's flesh with the same intense, controlled passion that he directs toward eating at Christians' expense, or parting with an improvident servant to accelerate the decline of Bassanio. It is the sure way to profit that Shylock goes about.

And yet, his actions demonstrate a kind of gamble too. Shylock's gamble is that he will lose his interest if Antonio's voyages suffer no series of disaster. It may be argued that in the event Shylock will "gain" Antonio's

133

friendship. Actors like to extract the utmost human sympathy out of the part, by suggesting that Shylock's decision to demand the pound of flesh comes later. On this interpretation, it is the flight of Jessica that raises his hatred to a frenzy. But I prefer to take at face value Jessica's unequivocal testimony: she had heard her father swear to Tubal and Chus he would rather have Antonio's flesh than twenty times the sum owed. (III, 2, 284-290) This, together with the aside of I, 3, 37-43, surely takes Shylock's intentions in I, 3 out of the realms of ambiguity. He risks a relatively small sum, the interest on his money, against a very great psychological satisfaction should Antonio miscarry.

The full extent of that gain is measurable, up to a point. If Antonio comes to grief, Shylock is in effect ready to pay 3,000 ducats for the body. It is a pure humor of hate:

> You'll ask me why I rather choose to have
> A weight of carrion flesh than to receive
> Three thousand ducats. I'll not answer that,
> But say it is my humor. Is it answered?
> What if my house be troubled with a rat,
> And I be pleased to give ten thousand ducats
> To have it baned? What, are you answered yet?
> Some men there are love not a gaping pig,
> Some that are mad if they behold a cat,
> And others, when the bagpipe sings i'th'nose,
> Cannot contain their urine; for affection,
> Master of passion, sways it to the mood
> Of what it likes or loathes. Now for your answer:

As there is no firm reason to be rend'red
Why he cannot abide a gaping pig,
Why he a harmless necessary cat,
Why he a woollen bagpipe, but of force
Must yield to such inevitable shame
As to offend himself being offended;
So can I give no reason, nor I will not,
More than a lodged hate and a certain loathing
I bear Antonio, that I follow thus
A losing suit against him.

(IV, 1, 40-62)

The "losing suit" phrase is, I think, especially significant.
It is usually taken to refer to the 3,000 ducats. It means
that, of course; but it must mean more. Shylock cannot
be unaware of the probable consequences of winning his
case, even of contesting it. Some form of personal disaster for him must lie in the wake of Antonio's death. Yet
his hatred drives him along a path that can only lead to
self-destruction, or mutual destruction. Even the uncouth
imagery of this speech shows his awareness of this truth.
"As to offend himself being offended" is the phrase that
lingers. (I think it an editorial error to place a comma
after "offend." The sense is that Shylock *offends himself*.) This line, together with the "losing suit," makes it
plain that Shylock accepts his own destruction as the
likely price for pulling Antonio down.

What the trial scene exhibits, then, is a savage ikon
of human relationships. Oddly, the underlying sense of
the transaction is better rendered in the language than
(often) on the stage. We speak habitually of someone

exacting "his pound of flesh." The tired metaphor communicates a truth that stage melodrama, with its ogreish knife-sharpening, may not. For the two main participants are frozen into a posture, however exaggerated and contorted, in which at some time all find themselves; debtor and creditor, exploiter and exploited meet to resolve their relationship. But the special satisfactions of that relationship are not to be limited to the nominal form, the apparent rights and wrongs of the situation. Shylock will be paid with Antonio's body, Antonio with giving his body to pay Bassanio's debt. Each will be paid, not in money, but in kind. The trial scene projects two sorts of creditor, two accomplices in the subterranean drama of exploitation and satisfaction.

VII

"Venture" and "thrift," then, attain their resolution in the trial scene. Via "hazard" ("Before you hazard . . . Before you venture for me" III, 2, 2 . . . 10), these terms modulate into the casket scenes, and thus into the world of Belmont. At Belmont, certain other words within the key group are given special emphasis. They are "lottery," "Fortune," "hazard." Now the general implication of these terms is that collectively they emphasize the notion of chance, that is, of high risk. Operations which are "filtered" by these terms may be regarded as largely outside the realm of calculation. It is this which serves to distinguish the idea of gain, in Belmont, from that prevailing in Venice.

This is most obviously seen in "lottery." The term is applied to the casket test set up by Portia's father:

Nerissa refers to "the lott'ry that he hath devised" (I, 2, 27-28), and Portia to "the lott'ry of my destiny." (II, 1, 15) Still, the apparent implication of random chance is not really present. The casket challenge is a form of selection technique, and Nerissa says as much: "Therefore the lott'ry that he hath devised in these three chests of gold, silver, and lead—whereof who chooses his meaning chooses you—will no doubt never be chosen by any rightly but one who you shall rightly love." (I, 2, 27-31) The lottery cannot be won by the wrong man. It is natural for the suitors, however, to appeal to "Fortune," and this they regularly do. "Fortune" is a fluid term. As first used by Nerissa, it suggests inherited wealth. (I, 2, 4) Morocco (who does not recognize the selection test aspect of the matter) regards the casket choice as an effect of "blind Fortune" unrelated to his deserts, and compares the entire operation with a dice throw. (II, 1, 31-38) At other times "Fortune" conveys its usual implications of "Fate," or "good fortune," and it is in this latter sense that Arragon invokes Fortune. (II, 9, 18)

"Hazard" is the chief manifestation of the "risk" notion. It figures in the lead casket motto: "Who chooseth me, must give and hazard all he hath." The context is love, and the meaning plain: to gain all, one must risk all. But Morocco balks at the fence:

> men that hazard all
> Do it in hopes of fair advantages.
> A golden mind stoops not to shows of dross,
> I'll then nor give nor hazard all for lead.
>
> (II, 7, 18-21)

137

Similarly Arragon: "You shall look fairer ere I give or hazard." (II, 9, 21) Bassanio has already, in his arrow-shoot metaphor, envisaged the wooing as a "hazard" (I, 1, 151), and is thus temperamentally attuned to the challenge of the lead motto. (The prime, virtually the only reason he gives for the choice is a suspicion of the gold motto.) "Hazard," then, is love in action. It is to be distinguished from the certainty (or calculated probability) of gain in the world of commerce, as also from that policy of calculated gain that Morocco and Arragon exhibit. Nevertheless, the distinction is one of emphasis. "Hazard" and "thrive" refuse to be totally dissociated, and "venture" links with both. The frontiers of Venice and Belmont are blurred; the worlds of commerce and love use each other's terms as a frame of reference.

How does this incline us toward Portia, and the Belmont values? The central Belmont impulse, plainly, differs from Venice's; yet there is no absolute antithesis; "hazard" and "venture" refuse to polarize. I see no ideal world of Belmont, no paradise-prototype (in spite of what Jessica says of its chatelaine, III, 5, 66-76, a panegyric that has a clear psychological context). Nor am I inclined toward a full-scale ironic interpretation of Portia, as A. D. Moody has advanced. In general terms, of course, Portia makes a glowing and distinguished impression. She is noble, witty, generous. Any attack on her, to be successful, must I think seize on the commercial imagery that (like virtually everyone else in the play) her words exhibit. Does this imagery reveal a mind too closely attuned to commerce? We might take this line as a crucial instance of the issues involved:

138

Portia: Since you are dear bought, I will love you dear.

(III, 2, 313)

There is nothing exceptional about this line; but it raises in acute form the problems of interpretation that the critic, and the actress, must face. I can see three ways of interpreting this line.

(i) Idealist: i.e., the actress may indicate that she is putting inverted commas around "bought." Portia is then aware of the commercial imagery, and distancing herself from it. "Dear" refers primarily to the intense emotional stress that keeping silent has meant for her. "Bought" is a mild joke, and she expects that Bassanio will have the wit and understanding to appreciate it.

(ii) Realist. Here we recognize a hard-headed heiress, coolly shopping for her male, who is fully aware of the literal implications of "bought"—and accepts them. This is not totally incompatible with (i)—the actress may indicate that it is a jest, but with an edge—still, the distinction in emphasis is perfectly clear.

(iii) Objective. In this reading one accepts that everyone in Venice-Belmont has a mind structured by commercial imagery, to whom expression via certain metaphors comes naturally. Hence one might base an interpretation of Portia on the broads lines of her part, and make nothing special of her commercial phraseology at all. Portia has simply assimilated the metaphors, is even unaware of them.

All of these possibilities deserve serious consideration. But they don't stand up equally well to scrutiny. (ii) is tempting, and has been performed after this fashion at

139

the highest level. But the part resists cynicism. If Portia really intends to acquire her preferred suitor, why not simply transmit the casket secret to Bassanio? Yet it is plain from her anguished suspense during Bassanio's soliloquy, especially in "O love, be moderate, allay thy ecstasy,/In measure rain thy joy, scant this excess" (III, 2, 111-112), that Portia is genuinely in doubt as to the outcome. She abides by her own and her father's rules. The casket problem, one has to point out, is a test of Portia, not merely of the suitors. She passes it.

(iii) is perhaps more plausible. It has the engaging advantage of offering a ready solution to the actress who can perceive no difficulties in "dear bought," or "My mind was never yet more mercenary" (IV, 1, 416), or "That only to stand high in your account,/I might in virtues, beauties, livings, friends,/Exceed account. But the full sum of me/Is sum of something." (III, 2, 155-158) The basic objection to this approach—and this one need not argue in detail—is that Portia is obviously, and preeminently, intelligent. It is surely a donnée of the part that Portia is aware of her own metaphors. It is an aspect of her tact. So "bought," "mercenary," "sum" would be crass and offensive terms, were they not neutralized and elevated to a high level of civilized intercourse by her understanding and courtesy.

So (i) remains. And this, I conclude, is the best interpretation. Not only does this reading suit the part, it accords with one's grasp of the play. It will be clear that I do not minimize the latent irony in *The Merchant of Venice*, and its quite remorseless exposure of human motivation and pretences. All the more important, therefore, is a resting point for one's emotions and sense of values. Portia is the countermovement to the general drift of *The Merchant of Venice*. Remove her, and the play might be a subtler version of *Volpone*. Modify her lineaments fractionally, and the terrible irony of the piece is overwhelming. As she is, Portia is the stable center of values, to which the action relates. It is, of course, the classic role for a Shakespearean heroine, and the parallels are convincing in themselves (Viola, Imogen, the Princess of France). Portia has to be able to ask for mercy and for judgment; and she has to be the one person in the play who can do it, without evoking either mockery or outrage.

VIII

Bassanio, oddly, stands up rather well to scrutiny. One has to avoid a facile cynicism in appraising him, and instead approach him with the iron objectivity that Shakespeare does. We can consider first the whole question of making a rich marriage. The action depicted in this play simply elaborates an ancient adage: do not marry for money, but marry where money is. I see no point in blaming Bassanio for pursuing this policy. He appears perfectly sincere in his protestations of love, and there is no reason to doubt his attachment to a goddess combining beauty, wealth, and love. Then there is the casket choice. Here again the question is crucial: if it can be established that Bassanio was given the secret of the caskets, our whole assessment of Belmont collapses. Critics have suspected, certainly, that the "head," "bred" rhymes in the song constitute a broad hint to Bassanio.

141

Directors may take up the hint in a production. Yet there is nothing at all in the preceding dialogue that constitutes hard evidence; nor does the dialogue, or song, plausibly initiate the train of thought emerging in Bassanio's "*So may the outward shows be least themselves.*" (III, 2, 73)

I should prefer to read Bassanio's soliloquy as evidence of his basic shrewdness, rather than of collusion or rational induction. It can, I think, be reasonably argued that gold, silver, and lead are self-evidently emblems; that gold and silver ("ornament") naturally make the point that Bassanio is quick to seize on, in his opening line. The caskets are emblems rather than arcane riddles, and communicate their point readily to a shrewd and receptive mind. Bassanio has antennae, he has "feel" for a situation. This, I suggest, is the secret of his success. And in one metaphor he reveals the contrast with Antonio: "Thus ornament is but the guiled shore/To a most dangerous sea . . ." (III, 2, 97-98) Antonio's ships are headed for that guiled shore; Bassanio's sense the danger and steer for safety. It is the difference between the loser and the winner.

IX

We need neither romanticize nor pillory Bassanio. What he hazards is other people's money, but he is perfectly open about it. (III, 2, 257-261) The irony that is latent in the action, and demands manifest expression, surfaces in the figures of his fellow suitors. They have no life beyond the casket scenes, hence the limits of their choice reduce them to stereotypes. They appear as caricatures of social attitudes. Morocco is the gold-man, identifying himself with the casket of his choice: "A golden mind stoops not to shows of dross." (II, 7, 20) For him, appearances are reality. Arragon is the pride-man, pluming himself on that merit, belonging naturally to him but alas usurped in others:

O that estates, degrees, and offices
Were not derived corruptly, and that clear honor
Were purchased by the merit of the wearer!
(II, 9, 40-42)

Yet his own title constitutes his sole claim to recognition. One can take this as simple fun, or black satire on the values of the Christian society as a whole. On this line of approach, one would group Arragon and Morocco with Shylock; that is, the social satire is rendered less apparent by translation into foreign modes. All three directly or obliquely criticize certain attitudes current in society. They are masks, with Shylock a highly realistic one. So the case for regarding all profit-making as legitimate is argued by a singularly repellent Jew; Mammon shows a black face, and Pride is a Spaniard. No offense in the world. This is why we ought, I believe, to restrain any impulse to denounce Portia and Bassanio as an heiress and adventurer in collusion. The success of a Shakespeare play depends quite considerably on the balance between the central and peripheral figures. The edge of the irony is reserved for the lesser figures.

This is plainly true of the Jessica-Lorenzo relationship. It is impossible not to feel the direction of Shakespeare's satire when Lorenzo, for example, exclaims "If e'er the Jew her father come to heaven,/It will be for his gentle daughter's sake." (II, 4, 33-34) This, after the news that Jessica is bringing Shylock's gold and jewels as dowry. Again, Jessica adopts a significant metaphor: "I will make fast the doors, and *gild myself*/With some moe ducats, and be with you straight." (II, 6, 49-50) Money seals relationships among the Venetians. And Jessica is rewarded by the frank comment of Gratiano, in whose coarseness of fiber is to be discerned the lowest common factor of the Venetians: "Now (by my hood) a gentle, and no Jew!" (II, 6, 51) To be received as an honorary Christian into this society, and for these reasons, is an event that defeats complacency. On such occasions—and there are many more in the comedies than is generally conceded—the difference in posture between Shakespeare and Jonson appears minimal.

The form of *The Merchant of Venice*, so far as I can apprehend it, is a series of relationships that demonstrate the interdependence of the worlds of commerce and of the emotions. "Venture," "hazard," "thrive" are the means through which the dramatis personae define themselves; and we cannot, in the context of the whole play, assign to these terms a firmly literal or metaphoric status. The characters' sense of the terms shifts subtly from one frame of reference to the other. So the play presents an evolving analysis of personal gain, whether expressed through love, hate, or commercial acquisition. And the climactic event in these relationships is still the theatrical center, the trial scene. It is in this scene that the implications of gain and loss are most nakedly exposed, and most tellingly presented.

144

The challenge that the play presents is ultimately less one of analysis than of judgment. The problems of *The Merchant of Venice* come down to assessing the quality of irony in the piece. That it exists cannot be doubted. The central juxtaposition of love and commerce engenders its own ironies, whatever the treatment. But there is much room for dispute over the intensity and extent of the irony. I prefer to see as the chief characteristic of *The Merchant of Venice* the rigorous objectivity of its analysis. The nature of the transactions seems, at times, to demand that they be delineated with a thought more authorial emphasis, one implying an impulse of rejection or approval. One would like, perhaps, a little more guidance. Yet the author does not relax the severity of his detachment. The balance is held evenly, and we must judge for ourselves. The exposure of underlying motivations (especially of Antonio) is, as I contend, formidable. It is nonetheless true to say, as one says at school, that Antonio is a good man risking his life for his friend, and that Portia and Bassanio are attractive young people who love each other. The melodrama is true, and the irony is true. This play can hold all the understanding of human conduct, at whatever level, that we bring to it.

CHAPTER VII

The Revengers' Comedy

A certain quality of brutality distinguishes *The Merry Wives of Windsor*. This derives from the circumstances of its composition: the old tale that the play was written upon demand within a short space of time is doubtless true, though one need not accept the Queen herself as the most exigent of the play's sponsors. It bears all the marks of rapid production, evident not so much in the loose ends and padding as in the forced and mechanical quality of the writing. The piece seems a by-product of Shakespeare's career, executed with professionalism but without inner commitment. To that extent, it does not appear to contribute organically to Shakespeare's development; and its dating is perhaps not an issue of the first order. I have no wish to contest William Green's very strong case[1] that *The Merry Wives of Windsor* was first performed in April 1597, and I accept that it appeared shortly after *Henry IV, Part II* and preceded *Henry V*.

The main problem of the commission is clearly the handling of Falstaff. It will not do to argue that *The Merry Wives of Windsor* is a totally different sort of play from the histories, and that its comic center bears no

---

[1] William Green, *Shakespeare's* "Merry Wives of Windsor" (Princeton, 1962).

relation, beyond the name, to the Falstaff of *Henry IV*. The first proposition is evidently true; the second ignores the facts of audience reaction. *The Merry Wives of Windsor* exists, and the Falstaff of that play exists, because its audience demanded more of Sir John and his retinue. The public could have been in no doubt that it was witnessing a further installment in the chronicles of Sir John. Besides, the modifications needed to adapt Falstaff to farce are not so great as is supposed. It is commonly said that Falstaff is much changed, that the Falstaff of *Henry IV* would have penetrated the deceptions without difficulty. Now this view is odd, because by the end of *Henry IV, Part II* Falstaff is living in an advanced state of fantasy. He has erected his hopes into facts, precisely the situation of *The Merry Wives of Windsor*. What has changed is not Falstaff, but other people. The environment no longer cooperates with him. Hal, in the Gadshill-Boar's Head escapade, is really an accomplice of Falstaff's, playing up to the old man. Elsewhere, as at Shrewsbury, Hal shields Falstaff from the consequences of his actions. The burghers of Windsor see matters differently. They, and not the declining Falstaff, make the play the brutal farce it is.

I

The idea of the play is revenge, a communal impulse of hostility directed toward a single target. The plot is a double revenge action. Mistress Ford's "How shall I be revenged on him? for revenged I will be, as sure as his guts are made of puddings" (ii, 1, 27-29) is echoed by Mistress Page's "How shall I be revenged on him?" (ii,

1, 59-60), the two uniting operatically in "Let's be revenged on him." (II, 1, 84) This move against Falstaff is preceded by Nym and Pistol's

Nym: I have operations which be humors of revenge.
Pistol: Wilt thou revenge?

(I, 3, 82-83)

And so the combination against Falstaff is mounted. The play essentially consists of "operations which be humors of revenge" against Falstaff, the comic scapegoat. Thus the moment which, more than any other, projects the idea of the play, is its climax. The play's ikon is the prostrate Falstaff, circled around (like a covered wagon by Indians), derided, pinched, and burnt by his tormentors.

The revenge motif unleashes much sadism in the audience. If farce were not mechanical, it would be Theater of Cruelty; so the playwright has to maintain his dramatis personae, and the audience's reactions, under rigorous control. Falstaff aside, the most vulnerable person in this farce-world is Ford. He has to have a capacity for feeling pain, the plot demands it. The part offers something to the actor, and has been known to stand stereoscopically out of a production. But the soliloquies of the apprehensive cornuto are not allowed to generate more than laughter, the laughter of rejection. The other characters fit into a consistent pattern, that of limitation. They normally exhibit a single humor, a quirk of attitude and language. No illustration is required, but we ought to note the reduction of this approach to characterization: the foreigners. Sir Hugh and Dr. Caius are distinguished for little save their un-Englishness: their accents place them, account for them, define them. They *are* accents. The difference between Fluellen and Sir Hugh is the measure of serious drama, and farce. The audience enjoys total superiority over these puppets, and this superiority extends to the situations in which they are placed. Time and again the audience has the advantage over the participants, and this is most tellingly, perhaps, demonstrated in the scenes between Falstaff and Ford/Brook. Falstaff's gifts as a raconteur compose what may be termed the manifest humor of III, 5. The dynamism of the encounter is situational; Ford, converting his horror to solicitude, is in a memorable plight, and nothing in the play is funnier than Falstaff's parting "Adieu. You shall have her, Master Brook; Master Brook, you shall cuckold Ford." (III, 5, 121-122) At such moments the audience enjoys a huge triumph at the expense of the participants in the action.

And this state of affairs is curiously reflected in IV, 1, the schooling of Will Page. No scene in the play is more readily dispensable; it is purely a review sketch. Yet the teacher-student relationship is analogous to the audience-actor situation: the audience is as superior to the Welsh pedagogue, quick to correct ("It is five *senses*. Fie, what ignorance is," I, 1, 156) as he is to William. The part, as so often in Shakespeare, implies the whole.

II

The quality of *The Merry Wives of Windsor* is perfectly expressed in its jokes. What *Pericles* is to myth, *The Merry Wives of Windsor* is to jokes; the piece is a Public Record Office of graffiti, a register of underground

149

jokes. Some of them, naturally, are harmless enough: the name joke, for instance ("Alice Shortcake," I, 1, 181), or Pistol's response to Falstaff's "My honest lads, I will tell you what I am about." "Two yards, and more." (I, 3, 35-36) But the play offers an opportunity, unparalleled in Shakespeare, to discern the underground life of the nation, surfacing briefly like the turbid Fleet before resuming its subterranean flow. Here, for example, are the comic foreigners whose insecure command of language leads to a scatological pun. *Dr. Caius*: "If dere be one, or two, I shall make-a de turd." (III, 3, 208) Here is that stock property of medical farce, or of farce containing a doctor, the bedpan joke:

Host: Thou art a Castilian King-Urinal (II, 3, 29)
Evans: I will knog his urinals about his knave's
costard.

(III, 1, 13-14)

Here is the combination of malapropism and pun scatological, or pun sexual: Mistress Quickly reigns over these provinces of language. "She's as fartuous a civil modest wife" (II, 2, 89-90) instances the one. The other is richly elaborated in IV, 1, where the audience is invited to share the commentary of Mistress Quickly on the grammar lesson. She, for the moment, is the representative of the audience on the stage. Without her, someone might conceivably miss the point of

Evans: What is the focative case, William?
William: "O, vocativo, O."
Evans: Remember, William; focative is "caret."

150

Any such strays are reintegrated into the community following Mistress Quickly's "And's that a good root." (IV, 1, 43-46) Nobody could miss the ensuing passage, with Mistress Quickly to establish the facts of the case:

Evans: What is your genitive case plural, William?
William: Genitive case?
Evans: Ay.
William: "Genitivo, horum, harum, horum."
Quickly: Vengeance of Jenny's case! fie on her! Never name her, child, if she be a whore.
Evans: For shame, 'oman.
Quickly: You do ill to teach the child such words. He teaches him to hick and hack, which they'll do fast enough of themselves, and to call "horum." Fie upon you!

(IV, 1, 49-58)

A bawd's speciality is bawdry: and Mistress Quickly's function is to deliver it, whether knowingly or not. ("She does so take on with her men—they mistook their erection." "So did I mine," says Falstaff bitterly. III, 5, 34-36) Inventive as some of the verbal humor is, most of the jokes exploit areas of stock response. The well-known addiction of the Irish to whiskey, and the Welsh to cheese, is faithfully noted. (II, 2, 272-275; V, 5, 79-80) Similarly, the Host's "bully-rook" and Nym's "humour" are a sort of inverted euphuism, a form of language that reduces all expression to a set mode. The Host has some feeling for language, but Nym's "humour" is pure catchphrase, and Shakespeare milks it shamelessly in I, 3. The solecisms of the undereducated (Slender and Quickly),

151

and the blunders of the foreigners are remorselessly detailed. Even the village idiot makes his contribution, through Simple's brief appearance. Double entendre reigns over all. The audience—whose faculties are less extended than in any other play in the canon—is consistently urged to celebrate its release from the standards normally operating in a Shakespeare comedy.

The jokes, the characters, and the action all express a central impulse: hostility governed by superiority. As is the audience to the mechanized puppets, so are the puppets to their target. And yet, Falstaff is not the only one to suffer, for the spirit of hostility, let loose in the play, turns round to strike back at its agents. The Host fools Sir Hugh and Dr. Caius, yet is robbed by the German confidence ring. Page deceives his wife concerning his daughter, yet is himself deceived by Fenton. Mistress Page triumphs over Falstaff, yet her plans for Anne are thwarted. Ford and his wife are presumably sufficiently paid by remaining married to each other; the record is fairly explicit on the matter. Everyone, it seems, is undercut. So revenge becomes a kind of figure for the impulse of hostility that animates the play; and that impulse is satisfied, in the audience, by the downfall of the revengers, just as it is at the end of *The Revenger's Tragedy*. (That, too, is an essentially comic resolution.) The balancing, or compensation of hostile forces is well observed by Falstaff, speaking for the audience: "I am glad, though you have ta'en a special stand to strike at me, that your arrow hath glanced." (v, 5, 221-222) This kind of resolution is one of comedy's analogues to catharsis.

The festive ending of *The Merry Wives of Windsor*, therefore, is not a jovial drunkenness, a feeling of holiday repletion, but the satisfaction of contending forces finding an equilibrium. It is the ideal ending for what, if one were to take it at all seriously, would be a markedly unpleasant play. One imagines that Shakespeare laid down his pen with some relief, after disposing of this account of ignorant stereotypes clashing by night. There are times, certainly, when on the evidence here one could mistake Shakespeare's avocation for scriptwriter, rather than playwright. All the same, one comes away from *The Merry Wives of Windsor* with a feeling of enhanced respect for its author. Only a professional could have done it.

CHAPTER VIII

Problems of Knowing

Much Ado About Nothing serves as well as any play to mark the useful limits of analyses confined to imagery. On *Much Ado*, Clemen has nothing to say; and Caroline Spurgeon indicates only the images of swift movement, of sport, and of nature.[1] Now these observations add up to a perfectly fair critical comment, that the play's atmosphere suggests sparkling contention in an essentially outdoors and reassuringly normal environment. But this comment does not provide a clue to the play's mechanism. The approach to *Much Ado* through language is, seemingly, closed or inhibited by Ifor Evans' verdict: ". . . *Much Ado* has thus no new approach to language, in the verse, nor any of that continuity of intention in the imagery, discovered already in *The Two Gentlemen of Verona* and in *A Midsummer Night's Dream* . . ."[2]

But a linguistic approach, of a sort, is perfectly feasible. One has only to consult the concordance to establish what, in the most basic sense, is *there*. The statistics of the word-frequencies offer a clear guide to the play's

[1] Caroline Spurgeon, *Shakespeare's Imagery* (Cambridge, 1935), pp. 263-266.

[2] B. Ifor Evans, *The Language of Shakespeare's Plays* (London, 1952), p. 110.

concerns. The usual eliminations can be made. Words that are purely syntactical necessities—"have," "shall," and so on—can be dismissed. A couple of very common words—"man," and "good"—need not detain us. We then arrive at what is generally understood, that the most frequently used significant word in *Much Ado*, as in the comedies generally, is "love." Since love is the subject matter of all the comedies, and has been extensively analyzed by John Russell Brown in his book on Shakespeare's comedies,[3] I pass by this word without more comment. It simply indicates that two of *Much Ado*'s three actions are explicitly about love. We then arrive at what is not generally understood, that the second most frequently occurring of the significant words is the verb "to know."

"Know," in all its forms ("knowest," "knows," and so on) occurs 84 times in *Much Ado*. Granted that this is a common enough verb, and that characters on the stage will always be asking each other questions as "Knowst thou this man?," 84 still seems an excessive number. And this impression is confirmed if we check with the plays immediately preceding and succeeding *Much Ado* in the canon. *A Midsummer Night's Dream* has 31; *The Merchant of Venice*, 60; *Henry IV* Parts I and II, 55 and 48; *Henry V*, 61; *The Merry Wives of Windsor*, 65; and *As You Like It*, 58. At this period of his life, Shakespeare's use of the word reaches a peak in *Much Ado*. The con-

---

[3] John Russell Brown, *Shakespeare and His Comedies* (London, 1957). Paul A. Jorgensen finds a special significance in the play's title, and argues strongly for the importance of "nothing." See Paul A. Jorgensen, *Redeeming Shakespeare's Words* (Berkeley and Los Angeles, 1962), pp. 22-42.

clusion is inescapable: 84 references denotes no mere statistical curiosity, but an important area of Shakespeare's concern in *Much Ado*. The simple word "know"—so banal, so profound—is a major part of the play's verbal texture, and the key to its structure. I now propose to relate this element of the verbal texture to the structure, so far as it can be discerned, of the play.

"Structure" is always, in Shakespeare, a difficult concept. This is apparent if one tries to apply the concept in the simplest possible way, by analyzing the plot of *Much Ado*. Even on this primitive matter, the critical consensus breaks down. For example, John Dover Wilson sees the play as having only two plots, Hero-Claudio and Benedict-Beatrice.[4] He has virtually nothing to say of the Dogberry scenes, and sees them simply as comic business, not plot. This is the position of M. C. Bradbrook, also a believer in "two plots"[5] plus "straight comic relief."[6] But John Wain, while seeing the play as starting out with two plots, regards them as Hero-Claudio and Dogberry-Verges.[7] For him, the central plot then emerges as Benedict-Beatrice, "that make[s] the operatic main plot seem absurdly unreal, and thus makes the Dogberry plot curve away into its own isolation. The play falls into three pieces." Such a view, rejecting the thematic unity of *Much Ado*, is not A. P. Rossiter's. While insist-

[4] John Dover Wilson, *Shakespeare's Happy Comedies* (London, 1962), p. 122.

[5] M. C. Bradbrook, *Shakespeare and Elizabethan Poetry* (London, 1951), p. 180.

[6] *Ibid.*, p. 188.

[7] John Wain, *The Living World of Shakespeare* (Harmondsworth, England, 1964), p. 94.

ing on the presence of three plots, he detects the essential relevance of the Dogberry scenes: "But misprison and misapprehension are present here too, in a different guise."[8] On the whole J. R. Brown is in agreement: while speaking of "the twin stories of *Much Ado About Nothing*,"[9] he recognizes that "the introduction of Constable Dogberry and the men of his watch, also contributes to presenting and widening the underlying theme of the whole play."[10] In sum, the critics quoted do not agree on the number of plots, on the identity of the "main" plot, or on the relevance of the Dogberry scenes. Those who claim a structural relevance for the Dogberry scenes (and this is the view I accord with) are obliged to recognize a theme which is articulated in all three of the actions, and which is thus advanced in nearly all of the scenes.

On this line of approach, then, we must think of the play's structure as manifest in a series of episodes, or rather situations, which have the status of variations on a theme. But what is the nature of these "situations," and how can we characterize them? Bertrand Evans' line is at first attractive; the essential device for him, is the "practice," and he notes: "All the action is impelled by a rapid succession of 'practices'—eight in all."[11] A practice is a deliberate attempt to foster error. But an important part of *Much Ado* consists of gratuitous falling into error; and another important part is the correct assess-

[8] A. P. Rossiter, *Angel with Horns* (London, 1961), p. 76.
[9] Brown, *op.cit.*, p. 118.
[10] *Ibid.*
[11] Bertrand Evans, *Shakespeare's Comedies* (Oxford, 1960), p. 69.

157

ment of truth, some of which process is embodied in quite minor passages. "Error," whether provoked or not, will simply not cover the activities of *Much Ado*. Suppose, then, that we conceive of the theme of *Much Ado* as an exploration of the limits and methods of knowledge. Such a conception allows us to shift the emphasis from the motives and techniques of instilling error, to the re-actions of the dramatis personae in assessing these phe-nomena. It enables us to seek the principle of the play's unity in a number of very varied scenes. In all this the word "know" acts as a small, insistent reminder of the target of the play's probing.

We can conveniently consider the play's "situations" (this is much better than "scenes") as falling into three groups: those which originate from "practice"; those which afford without previous direction a source of error or revelation of truth; and those which dramatize a sift-ing of evidence, an assessment of appearance and reality.

I

The eight practices in *Much Ado* are best regarded as stimuli to provoke interesting reactions. They are not, in themselves, interesting events; and the most notable of the practices, the deception of Don Pedro and Claudio, takes place off stage. Moreover, Shakespeare develops no study of the motivation of the practicers. The practices are of two sorts, benevolent and malevolent. The benevo-lent ones have as motive the tautology of well-wishing; there is no more to say. The malevolence of Don John is a study deferred, for some half-dozen years, until Iago can provide a suitable dramatic focus. In this play Shakespeare declines to be drawn into a prolonged analysis of evil, and presents Don John purely as a sketch: "it must not be denied but I am plain-dealing villain." (I, 3, 27-28) To speak, therefore, of the quantity of "deceit" in *Much Ado* is misleading. "Deceit" is an active word, and the dramatic interest lies elsewhere than in the activators of deception.

The point need not be labored, but some important illustrations are worth citing. Thus, Claudio's reaction to Don's John's report that Don Pedro is enamoured of Hero is typical:

Claudio: How know you he loves her?
Don John: I heard him swear his affection.
Borachio: So did I too, . . .
Claudio: Thus answer I in name of Benedick
But hear these ill news with the ears of
Claudio.
'Tis certain so. The prince woos for himself.
Friendship is constant in all other things
Save in the office and affairs of love.
Therefore all hearts in love use their own
tongues;
Let every eye negotiate for itself
And trust no agent; . . .
(II, 1, 149-161)

Naturally this exchange reveals Claudio's uncertainty and inclination to jealousy. But there is an underlying point. Claudio asks for the sources of knowledge, and is told: the senses, the ear. He then abjures all intermediaries and places his faith in sensory knowledge—a means

159

of knowledge which, as we shall see, is quite inadequate. This is fully demonstrated in the practice played upon Benedick by Leonato, Claudio, and Don Pedro. The three discuss in Benedick's hearing Beatrice's love for him. Benedick, stupefied, hears every word clearly. There is no question of sensory deception. He must *assess* the situation. His first reaction is that old men are unlikely to play tricks—"I should think this a gull but that the white-bearded fellow speaks it." (II, 3, 115-116) Later he refers to the verisimilitude of the charade: "This can be no trick. The conference was sadly borne." (II, 3, 202-203) Beatrice, indeed, puts up even less resistance in the parallel scene. She, and Benedick, are both right and wrong. Their judgment of the overheard conversations, a matter primarily of the senses, is at fault; their underlying grasp of the truth of the report is surely sound. As it happens, both have excellent intuitive judgment—a fact borne out elsewhere. But in this specific instance, their senses have certainly misled them.

And this is at the heart of the play's central error. Don John, laying charges against Hero's honor, offers to provide "evidence" of the senses: "If you will follow me, I will show you enough; and when you have seen more and heard more, proceed accordingly." Claudio responds on the same level, emphasizing (as before) the eye: "If I see anything to-night why I should not marry her to-morrow, in the congregation where I should wed there will I shame her." (III, 2, 108-110).

This position leads Claudio logically to his denunciation of Hero. Preceded by a tremolo on "know"—the Friar, by virtue of his office, asks the question that

launches "know" on a minor flurry of repetition—
Claudio delivers his speech on "seeming." (IV, 1, 28-
40) And his affirmation of knowledge comes down to
"Are our eyes our own?" (IV, 1, 69) In this he is backed
up by Don Pedro: "Myself, my brother, and this grievèd
Count/Did see her, hear her, . . ." (IV, 1, 87-88) The
senses, without judgment, are seen to be useless.

The point is underlined by Leonato's behavior. He
takes his profusion of blushes as evidence of guilt:
"Could she here deny/The story that is printed in his
blood? (IV, 1, 119-120) Beatrice's absence from Hero's
bedchamber evokes "Confirmed, confirmed!" (IV, 1,
148) And finally, his judgment rests on the standing of
other people: "Would the two princes lie?" (IV, 1, 150)
His method of confirming evidence is grossly at fault,
and is at odds with his cool and skeptical reception of
the servant's news in I, 2.

The true value here is provided by the Friar. He, like
the others, has used his eyes, "By noting of the lady."
(IV, 1, 156) But he relies not only on his senses, but on
his experience of life. His judgment is sounder; and better still, he has a sounder method, for the matter will
need to be put to further tests. Hence his key statement
of the knowledge-method:

Trust not my reading nor my observations,
Which with experimental seal doth warrant
The tenure of my book; . . .
If this sweet lady lie not guiltless here
Under some biting error.

              (IV, 1, 163-165 . . . 167-168)

161

"Experimental seal" is the test of knowledge. And this thought is allowed to penetrate even the following passage, the coming together of Beatrice and Benedick. The heart of it is:

Benedick: I do love nothing in the world so well as you. Is not that strange?
Beatrice: As strange as the thing I know not.

(IV, 1, 264-266)

How, indeed, can Beatrice "know" in the full sense what her instinct assures her to be the truth? Her own version of the "experimental seal" follows shortly: "Kill Claudio." (IV, 1, 285) Several points converge in this terse imperative other than the purely theatrical. It is a version of "If you love me, *then* prove it." Moreover, the issue is symbolic. "Kill Claudio" is to kill the Claudio in oneself—to kill the force of distrust. It is to yield to the value of trust, formed on a sufficient appraisal of another, and implicit faith. In a word, it is to love. Beatrice will accept nothing less, and Benedick—after a decent hesitation—is right to grant it.

The practices, then, initiate a series of situations in which the victims regularly cooperate in their own gulling. Their senses play no tricks; but reliance on the senses, without reference to the controls of judgment, experience, and method simply defines a limit of knowledge.

II

Certain situations arise in which error, or revelation of truth, occur without being consciously provoked.

These extend the range of tests to which the dramatis personae are exposed. Such a test occurs in the play's second scene; really it is two situations compressed into a tiny, but important episode. First, there is the servant's overhearing of the Claudio-Don Pedro conversation. He reports that the Prince has confessed his love for Hero. The man, plainly, has heard perfectly correctly—as a glance at the preceding scene demonstrates. A line such as "And in her bosom I'll unclasp my heart" (I, 1, 291) is, taken in isolation, extremely suggestive. But the man has heard only a fragment of the conversation, taken out of context, and thus has totally misconstrued it. The second situation is the contrasted reaction of Leonato and Antonio. Antonio is inclined to lend the report some credence, but willing to wait upon the event; Leonato is more skeptical, demanding corroboratory evidence:

Antonio: But, brother, I can tell you strange news that
you yet dreamt not of.
Leonato: Are they good?
Antonio: As the event stamps them; but they have a
good cover, they show well outward. . . .
Leonato: Hath the fellow any wit that told you this?
Antonio: A good sharp fellow. I will send for him, and
question him yourself.
Leonato: No, no. We will hold it but a dream till it
appear itself; . . .

(I, 2, 3-7 . . . 15-19)

Leonato's attitude here is at variance with his later behavior. His unwillingness to interrogate (brought out in the church scene, and his refusal to preside over the

163

examination of Conrade and Borachio) fixes a standard of improper conduct.

The following scene (i, 3) between Don John and his minions provides a neat inversion of the theme. Error has been allowed to grow into proven truth, or no: now truth—Borachio has heard the Claudio-Don Pedro dialogue quite correctly—is promoted to foster error. Leonato, "no hypocrite, but prays from his heart" (i, 1, 135), yields place in the patterned maneuvering to Don John, "I cannot hide what I am: . . . I am a plain-dealing villain." (i, 3, 11 . . . 28) But the situation is grasped and developed with a malignant competence. Knowledge, in *Much Ado* is largely the property of the villains and clowns. The intelligent sophisticates miss it most of the time.

The clowns receive their windfall in iii, 3. Since Borachio and Conrade expose themselves fully to the listeners, there is no question of mishearing or misinterpretation. The actual process of revelation proceeds without obstacle. Apart from the clothes imagery of the Borachio-Conrade exchange ("Thou knowest that the fashion of a doublet, or a hat, or a cloak, is nothing to a man," iii, 3, 108-110) which classically embodies the idea of appearance-reality, there is little interest attached to the content of the revelation episode. The real point has emerged earlier, in the discussion of methods of detection employed by the Watch. This has to come before. It is useless afterwards, because there is no problem of comprehension involved in the drunken babbling of Borachio. The methods employed by the constabulary

164

will certainly survive scrutiny, if their command of language will not. We can note the chain of tests.

(1) Challenge any suspicious character: upon which, as Verges correctly observes, "If he will not stand when he is bidden, he is none of the Prince's subjects." (iii, 3, 29-30)

(2) "Make no noise in the streets." (iii, 3, 32-33) This is a sort of plain-clothes technique, in which trouble is allowed to raise its head.

(3) As for drunks, order them off to bed. If they are incapable "let them alone till they are sober. If they make you not then the better answer, you may say they are not the men you took them for." (iii, 3, 43-45)

(4) In the case of suspected thieves, the procedure is "Softly, softly." The Second Watchman has raised the issue with the question containing the key word: "If we know him to be a thief, shall we not lay hands on him?" And Dogberry's answer is a model of detective's circumspection: "Truly, by your office, you may; but I think they that touch pitch will be defiled. The most peaceable way for you, if you do take a thief, is to let him show himself what he is, and steal out of your company." (iii, 3, 53-56) In analysis, if not in performance, we should not allow ourselves to be taken in by the superb comedy of the trouble-shunning Watch and their majestic leader. In truth, a model procedure is outlined before us in the Watch's catechism. The logic of the procedure for detection is impeccable. In their system, a hypothesis must be checked against a sufficient body of confirmatory data. It is the true counterpart of the Friar's "experimental

165

seal." Their procedures make the Watch cousins-german to the man who, as T. W. Craik correctly observes, is the "new point of reference"[12] in the play. It is clear that the Watch's social superiors make a basic error in detection and apprehension: that of striking too soon.

In fine, the Watchman's discovery of Borachio and Conrade rounds off a series of three casual and unforced overhearings. Knowledge has been supplied to the sophisticates, the villains, and the clowns. This, in two of the three instances, has served as peg for disquisitions on the methods of securing knowledge, of confirming likely hypotheses. These discussions link the situations with those provoked by the practices. And the true model for these occasions emerges from Dogberry's words (as, from the practices, it emerges from the Friar's). Malapropism is not a comic extravaganza, it is a central verbal device for presenting the play's theme. Dogberry's language is a burlesque of truth, but not a denial of it. His Watch, for all their naïveté and incompetence, have the root of the matter in them.

III

The eight practices and three overhearings provide a series of situation in which discussion of truth is, as it were, a formal necessity. These situations compose the framework of the plot. But they do not yield the total of the play's structure. *Much Ado* contains, in addition, several passages which lightly and flexibly extend the theme which has been uttered, and two set-pieces (the masque

[12] T. W. Craik, "*Much Ado About Nothing*," *Scrutiny*, XIX (1953), 314.

and the examination) which provide a symbol of the play's business. The extension of the play's concerns into the informal and openly symbolic reveals, I believe, Shakespeare's techniques even more clearly than the product of the foregoing analysis.

(i) We can perfectly well begin with the opening line of *Much Ado*: Leonato's "I learn in this letter." It is Shakespeare's habit to strike to the heart of the play's concerns as rapidly as possible. (For example, Harry Levin's study of *Hamlet*[13] is based on the idea that the play's conceptual structure, a question, is revealed in the opening line "Who's there?") One cannot, obviously, make too much of the necessary question-and-answer that speed an exposition. The news of the battle, and the status of the visitors, must be transmitted to the audience as soon as possible. Still, the opening lines suggest the underlying theme very well. The initial talk is of learning, of assessing people and faces. (I, 1, 18-26) Benedick's opening line presents theme-through-jest (the same technique that we have observed in the Dogberry scenes): "Were you in doubt, Sir, that you asked her?" (I, 1, 95) The opening episode ends with Don Pedro accepting the invitation to stay as genuine, since he judges Leonato to mean his words: "I dare swear he is no hypocrite, but prays from his heart." (I, 1, 135) In short, the opening passage has moved rapidly from the communication of factual knowledge to the problem of knowing people.

(ii) The matter is then developed into the colloquy between Benedick and Claudio, which follows immedi-

---

[13] Harry Levin, *The Question of Hamlet* (New York, 1961).

ately. The two friends have considerable difficulty in deciding how serious the other is. Claudio asks for Benedick's opinion of Hero, and receives an offhand jesting answer. Claudio, misconstrued, says: "Thou thinkest I am in sport. I pray thee tell me truly how thou lik'st her." (I, 1, 157-158) Benedick cannot decide the issue at all: "But speak you this with a sad brow? or do you play the flouting Jack?" (I, 1, 161-162) The problem of knowing when one's friend is in earnest is, for the moment, too much for these two.

(iii) The arrival of Don Pedro complicates and intensifies the discussion. The conversation now turns on the difficulties of assessing one's own feelings, as opposed to those of others. The distinctions are delicately separated.

Claudio: You speak this to fetch me in, my lord.
Don Pedro: By my troth, I speak my thought.
Claudio: And, in faith, my lord, I spoke mine.
Benedick: And by my two faiths and troths, my lord,
                       I spoke mine.
Claudio: That I love her, I feel.
Don Pedro: That she is worthy, I know.
Benedick: That I neither feel how she should be loved,
                       nor know how she should be worthy, is the
                       opinion that fire cannot melt out of me.
                                                           (I, 1, 198-207)

The alignment of "knowing" and "feeling" is the axis of the crucial scenes in Act IV. Intuition (sound) governing knowledge is the standard advanced later by Benedick and Beatrice; intuition allied to a proper experimental approach to knowledge is the even better synthesis proposed by the Friar. Claudio has no judgment and no method. The opening passages, then, reveal him ominously prepared to accept "love" as consequent upon the opinion of others; and as ominously, scattering the word "liked" in the midst of his talk of "love." (I, 1, 267, 268, 273, 282) To sum up, the play's opening passages parse the difficulties of knowing one's own feelings, and those of others. The key words are "know," "feel," "opinion," "think." This dialogue (I, 1) states the argument of the play.

(iv) The masque episode, as in *Love's Labour's Lost*, presents a central symbol. Now in *Much Ado*, the masque reveals a pattern of penetrated disguises, but no longer reflecting a simple male-female opposition. The center of interest is the key word "know," used 8 times in this short passage. Thus, Ursula and Antonio play an elegant variant on the tune:

Ursula: I know you well enough. You are Signor Antonio.

Antonio: At a word, I am not.

Ursula: I know you by the waggling of your head.

Antonio: To tell you true, I counterfeit him.

Ursula: You could never do him so ill-well unless you were the very man. Here's his dry hand up and down. You are he, you are he!

Antonio: At a word, I am not.

Ursula: Come, come, do you think I do not know you by your excellent wit? Can virtue hide itself?

                  (II, 1, 99-108)

169

Hypothesis yields to experimental confirmation. This badinage presents the stuff of the play as plainly as the better known passages in the "big" scenes. And Claudio, confronted by Don John, twice touches the telling word—once as a lie, once as a question directed toward a lie:

Don John: Are you not Signior Benedick?
Claudio: You know me well. I am he. . . . How know you he loves her?

(ii, 1, 143-144, 149)

Reduce the masque to its verbal core, and it resolves into two syntactic units; the statement, "I know you," and the question, "How do you know?" The texture of the dialogue—light, repeated references to "know"—suggests unmistakably the concept dominating the scene.

(v) The raillery of Act iii, Scene 2, keeps the theme going. Don Pedro and Claudio twit Benedick on his outward signs of love—his clothes, his melancholy, his beardless face, and so on. The talk is all of identifying Benedick's sickness from outward signs:

Claudio: If he be not in love with some woman, there is no believing old signs.

(iii, 2, 36-37)

And the matter is virtually formalized into the expected constellation of "knows":

Claudio: Nay, but I know who loves him.
Don Pedro: That would I know too. I warrant, one that knows him not.

(iii, 2, 56-58)

170

On the entry of Don John, the word becomes a trill—it is almost operatic:

Don John: Means your lordship to be married
             tomorrow?
Don Pedro: You know he does.
Don John: I know not that, when he knows what I
             know.   (III, 2, 77-80)

And he goes on to give his reasons. In this scene as elsewhere, "knowledge" is defined empirically—the concept is studied through the means of defining it.

(vi) The mirror image of the Don Pedro-Claudio examination of Benedick occurs in III, 4: Beatrice is quizzed by Margaret on the import of his "sickness"; and Margaret correctly diagnoses a state for which *Carduus Benedictus* is the cure. The conspirators, like their male counterparts, are in the know and have no difficulty in reading the signs. Dramatically, these two passages form a welcome relief from the situations in which the dramatis personae make much heavier weather of the business of assessing truth.

(vii) Yet again, the problem of assessing people concerns a minor but perfectly congruent passage. Benedick, convinced by Beatrice of Hero's innocence, comes to deliver the challenge to Claudio. Almost any other dramatist here would have made Benedick deliver the challenge briskly, concentrating on the powerful effect of the actual challenge of the speech. But not Shakespeare. He positively loiters over the passage, allowing Benedick the best part of a hundred lines between entrance and exit. (V, 1, 110-186) The passage is lengthened to provide

171

a quite different sort of interest; eventually it is a pro-longed test by Claudio and Don Pedro to discover if Benedick be in earnest or not. A series of maladroit jests, embarrassing in their oafishness, evokes only the same iron response from Benedick. The climax of the passage occurs not in the delivery of the challenge, but the unwilling realization of the jesters that Benedick really means it: Don Pedro's simple, deflated "He is in earnest" (v, 1, 187) acknowledges the truth that appearances (for once) do not deceive. Thus, the dialogue is constructed not so much to make an immediate theatrical point, as to extend further the fabric from which *Much Ado* is woven.

(viii) The examination of Borachio and Conrade by Dogberry and his minions is a set piece that restates and synthesizes the play's concerns. It blares forth with a stridency of brass and provocation of bassoon the theme of *Much Ado*. But take away the superb inanities of Dogberry and we are left with an implied comment. It is for the Watch to do the work neglected by their betters. Leonato, failing in this as in other business, has dele-gated his functions to Dogberry. The Watch—with intel-ligent help from the Sexton and Verges—pull their supe-rior through. It is precisely in this, the marshalling of evidence and formation of proper judgment, that the Watch succeeds and the others fail. To speak of these scenes as "comic relief" is to misjudge entirely Shake-speare's design. Borachio can see the point: "I have de-ceived even your very eyes" (so much for evidence based solely on the senses): "what your wisdom could not discover, these shallow fools have brought to light." (v, 1, 221-222)

The transposition of theme from serious to comic is, as always, a basic Shakespearean technique. The Dogberry scenes provide a remarkable instance of Shakespeare's easy command of material, that is, his capacity to pursue an idea throughout a play across scenes varying very widely in mood, dramatis personae, and (apparently) situation. It may well be, as many critics have suggested, that a vital stage in Shakespeare's development was marked by the arrival of Robert Armin with the company. In other words, the wise fools of the later comedies—Touchstone and Feste—depended for their creation on an actor of intelligence and distinction capable of projecting these demanding roles. This may well be, but I point out that such a step is perfectly implicit in the comic work in *Much Ado*. The difference between Dogberry (a part that does not demand an actor of intelligence) and Feste is one of consciousness. Feste knows his own significance to the main action, Dogberry does not. But that is the only difference. Shakespeare has planted Dogberry among the Messinans with a full awareness of his relevance: a parody of a reference-point, a Friar's zany.

We have, in sum, a number of passages, not directly connected with the practices or with the eavesdroppings, that relate the same fundamental situation. The situation poses always the question: how do I *know*? How can I be sure that *A* is telling the truth, that *B* is a villain, that *C* loves me, that *D* is lovesick? How can intuition be

173

confirmed? These variants of the central question are ex-
hibited, with complete formal mastery, in virtually every
scene in *Much Ado*.

As a convenience of analysis, I have separated the situations in *Much Ado* into three categories—those aris-
ing from practice, from chance, and from the necessities
of life as they occur. It is clear that they amount to variants of a single central situation: the problem of knowing. This problem is carefully delineated in *Much Ado*;
the metaphysical probings of *Hamlet* are, I believe, no-
where hinted at. The concern of the characters in *Much
Ado* is to determine from behavior the feelings and attitudes of the other characters. All other aspects of the
problem are excluded.

The idea of *Much Ado* is located in a commonplace
word, and not in a striking image; it has on that account
been largely overlooked in studies of the play. Yet the
numerous references to "know" (to which one can add
smaller groups of related words, "think," "believe,"
"sure") point unmistakably to Shakespeare's design. And
this is confirmed by situational analysis. "Know" is the
conceptual principle of the play.

And finally: "know" reveals the direction in which
Shakespeare is moving. Much of the ground in *Much
Ado* he traverses again in *Othello*. The essential difference between the two plays is the attention paid to the
problem of evil, as manifest in Iago and Othello—the
other problems of "knowing" are dealt with in much
the same way. The other, profounder, questions that relate to "know" are reserved for *Hamlet*. *Much Ado* is a
base camp that secures the approaches to the peak.

CHAPTER IX

No Exit from Arden

As You Like It I take to be a synthesis of two structures, that of romance and antiromance. The romantic elements need no recapitulation here; they compose, quite simply, the plot. Of the antiromantic elements, much has already been commented on. For example: Rosalind, Touchstone, and Jacques provide a running fire (within the spectrum realism-satire) on the posturing of the romantics. There are plenty of overt hints that Arden is no paradise. Touchstone's "Ay, now am I in Arden, the more fool I" (II, 4, 14) shades into the evocation, which Kott has noted,[1] of an agrarian system governed by the capitalist laws of hire:

> But I am shepherd to another man
> And do not shear the fleeces that I graze.
> My master is of churlish disposition.
>
> (II, 4, 73-75)

And the play's conclusion, a set of major cadences rung to wedding bells, has already been consistently minored by the many references—obsessive, even for an Elizabethan comedy—to the traditional aftermath of mar-

---

[1] Jan Kott, *Shakespeare Our Contemporary* (Garden City, New York, 1966), p. 329.

riage. The dwellers in Arden hear ever at their back the sound of horns.[2]

As You Like It's discordant music can be viewed as complementary to the play's evolving debate. It has become habitual to see the play's form as a set of debates. This is obviously true up to a point, though one should distinguish between the subject of the debate—usually Court versus country—and the grand theme, which is the romantic ideal challenged by the probings of realism, common sense, and satire. And yet the term "debate," useful though it is in identifying an aspect of the play's tradition and form, masks a trap. The word tends to connote a balanced and objective inquiry into truth, an analysis conducted under conventional rules of a subject in which the allocation of sides to speakers is without psychological commitment, an opportunity to display dexterity. Such an implication is misleading here; for Shakespeare presents the "debate" invariably as a struggle for mastery between two human beings, each of whom is determined to impose his or her values on the other. The constant human drive to dominate another is the underlying theme of much of the dialogue; and it is codified in Touchstone's haughty (and instant) response to Corin's "Who calls?" "Your betters, sir." (II, 4, 63) The power struggle, in muted form, is quite as present in Arden as at Court; and we should look for its presence throughout the play following its overt presentation in Act I, the usurpation and defense of power. In view of

[2] In sum: "Arden is not a place where the laws of Nature are abrogated and roses are without their thorns." Helen Gardner, "*As You Like It*," in *Shakespeare: The Comedies*, ed. Kenneth Muir (Englewood Cliffs, New Jersey, 1964), p. 65.

Shakespeare's capacity for fusing the literal and symbolic, I would not dismiss the wrestling match as a mere concession to the groundlings. On the contrary, the wrestling match is no bad figure for much of the play's substance. And I incline to regard the succession of covert struggles (to which we can return, in detail, later) as an extension of the play's antiromantic structure.

But we can go further than this in our recognition of the play's antiromantic possibilities, and I wish here to examine the relationships in *As You Like It*. Virtually all the relationships are governed by a sense of unease, irritation, or hostility. The impression we receive from the two major lovers in the foreground is quite different from that derived from the other relationships (which include Rosalind and Orlando when confronted by any but each other). Indeed, if we disregard these lovers, we can perceive that the keynote of the relationships is a subdued or overt irritation. The reasons for this groundswell of hostility I take to be threefold: an underlying recognition that other people's qualities parallel and subtly menace one's own; an open clash of temperament and of values; and a simple will to dominate. Let us consider the relationships in the light of these categories.

I

The opening act provides us with the essence of the matter. Act I of *As You Like It* is sometimes viewed as a mere necessity of plot construction, yet it is almost the fundamental error of Shakespeare interpretation to write off any aspect of his work as being imposed by external necessity of stagecraft. We encounter two figures who find certain relationships intolerable: Oliver and Duke Frederick. They present, obviously, the idea of conflict, but also prefigure the situation of insupportable relationship. Oliver, vis-à-vis Orlando, presents the first of these situations. His hatred is located in no known cause: ". . . for my soul, yet I know not why, hates nothing more than he." (I, 1, 151-153) And then, as Oliver continues to brood on the matter, the truth tumbles involuntarily out—this is a soliloquy, the repository if not the billboard of truth in Shakespeare:

> Yet he's gentle, never schooled and yet learned, full
> of noble device, of all sorts enchantingly beloved;
> and indeed so much in the heart of the world, and
> especially of my own people, who best know him,
> that I am altogether misprised.
>
> (I, 1, 153-157)

It looks forward to Iago's muttered charge against Cassio, "He hath a daily beauty in his life/That makes me ugly." (*Othello*, v, 1, 19-20) It is possible to dislike others because they caricature oneself; Oliver hates Orlando because *he* seems an inferior version of his golden brother. And Adam commits the unforgivable sin, not of supporting Orlando, but of witnessing the two brothers' confrontation: hence, "Get you with him, you old dog." (I, 1, 75) Whereupon Adam doubles his offence by pointing out that Oliver is also an inferior copy of his father. The trouble, for Oliver, is the audience: hell is other people.

Orlando, then, is hated for his excellence, a situation which Adam sees very clearly:

Your praise is come too swiftly home before you.
Know you not, master, to some kind of men
Their graces serve them but as enemies?

(II, 3, 9-11)

Duke Frederick, Oliver's parallel, may well be assumed
to share this hatred of his civilized and urbane brother.
His prevailing state of mind, as revealed, is characterized
by suspiciousness and insecurity. A usurper himself, he
sees threats everywhere. For him, the mere presence of
people who recall his past is intolerably disturbing.
Orlando, son of Sir Rowland, evokes only

I would thou hadst been son to some man else.
The world esteemed thy father honorable,
But I did find him still mine enemy.

(I, 2, 205-207)

Similarly, for Rosalind: "Thou art thy father's daughter,
there's enough." (I, 3, 54) The Duke is able to rational-
ize his dislike for Rosalind into

She is too subtile for thee; and her smoothness,
Her very silence and her patience,
Speak to the people, and they pity her.
Thou art a fool. She robs thee of thy name.

(I, 3, 73-76)

No doubt this situation objectively exists, but the Duke
is clearly oppressed by a sense of comparisons, fatal to
himself, suggested by the names of Sir Rowland, Orlando, Rosalind, Duke Senior. We should expect that
this awareness of self-comparison is continued into his
relationship with Oliver; and this is so. For obvious social

179

reasons, Oliver has no opportunity of expressing his opinion of his parallel, the Duke; but the Duke has. "More villain thou." (III, 1, 15)

The matter is analyzed more acutely in Act II, in the relationships radiating out from Jacques. We need for the moment to note two: with Duke Senior, and with Touchstone. Now Duke Senior is the only character who has established a position in which he is, psychologically, immune to threats. He is equable, urbane, an ideal philosopher. He is, however, presented as an incorrigible moralizer; he is not to be restrained from sermonizing on stones. He sees the exterior world as a series of emblems. But this is precisely the bent of Jacques' mind. Independently he and the Duke arrive at the same metaphor: they perceive the natural kingdom of Arden as a power struggle where man usurps the beasts' place, just as he himself is the victim of usurpation. (II, 1) The point is not only that they agree—thus helping to establish the theme of natural conflict—but that they parallel each other, thus creating a tension. This is not apparent in the Duke's words; he is, after all, the overlord, and a man of rare mental equilibrium. For him, Jacques is an object of instruction and diversion: "I love to cope him in these sullen fits,/For then he's full of matter." (II, 1, 67-68) Jacques, however, resents the patronage of a social superior whose mind inclines the same way as his. "And I have been all this day to avoid him. He is too disputable for my company. I think of as many matters as he, but I give heaven thanks and make no boast of them." (II, 5, 29-32) A palpable hit: Jacques, as we shall see, always flinches when touched. Here, at all events, we can note that the affinity between the Duke and Jacques (the tendency to dispute and moralize) results in the discomfort of the weaker man.

The mechanism of Jacques' relationships is detailed to us in II, 7. I find in it one of the central passages of the play. Jacques has just entered, crowing of his encounter with Touchstone: "A fool, a fool! I met a fool i' th' forest," and goes on to describe it. (II, 7, 12-34) We should note that the Touchstone reported here is unrecognizable as the Touchstone we encounter before our eyes. Jacques presents Touchstone to us as a "fool" in the double sense ("lack-lustre eye. . . . Says very wisely. . . .") whereas it is perfectly clear elsewhere that Touchstone is an extremely intelligent man. Jacques' note is one of sour disdain, of scorn for the object that dares to "moralize" (as he does). The word "fool" occurs 12 times in this speech; and the idea of the speech is the tension between the two senses of "fool," jester and simpleton. And why? The why, as Jacques would say, is plain as way to parish church. He goes on to generalize— and as usual, when he generalizes, he talks of himself. The connection between generality and application is perfectly plain, if implicit:

> He that a fool doth very wisely hit
> Doth very foolishly, although he smart,
> Not to seem senseless of the bob.
>
> (II, 7, 53-55)

The Duke's strong riposte (II, 7, 64-69) asserts that Jacques' generalizations have a personal origin and application; it must be so with "He that a fool doth very

181

wisely hit" as well. We need this passage to explain the major preceding speech, and much else in *As You Like It*. Jacques' relationship with Touchstone depends on this admission:

> When I did hear
> The motley fool thus moral on the time,
> My lungs began to crow like chanticleer
> That fools should be so deep-contemplative.
>
> (ii, 7, 28-31)

Touché: two fools together. Only Jacques does not say as much; he oscillates between a scornful wish (to the Duke) to be a fool ("Invest me in my motley," ii, 7, 58) and a consistent attempt to patronize Touchstone when they meet. He does not say to Touchstone "Motley's the only wear. . . ." (ii, 7, 34) It is far more important to Jacques to maintain the position of mental superiority—if he can.

Jacques, in short, finds himself caricatured by the moralizing fool. That Touchstone is a thoroughgoing professional adds to his offence. His response is a strategy of alternately deriding and patronizing Touchstone, which he pursues right up to the final scene: "Is not this a rare fellow, my lord? He's as good at anything, *and yet a fool.*" (v, 4, 98-99) Jacques is exhibiting his good taste as a connoisseur of virtuosi, not genuinely commending Touchstone. The real man breaks out in the sudden stab of rancor at the end. To only one couple does Jacques fail to be civil, and offer the conventional good wishes: "And you to wrangling, for thy loving voyage/Is but for two months victualled." (v, 4, 185-186)

There remains a final instance in this category. Rosalind, overhearing Phebe's rejection of Silvius, interrupts the conversation with quite astonishing warmth—and rudeness. Why so much heat? The point of Phebe's speech (III, 5, 8-27) is a ruthless exposition of the banal conceit advanced by Silvius:

'Tis pretty, sure, and very probable
That eyes, that are the frail'st and softest things,
Who shut their coward gates on atomies,
Should be called tyrants, butchers, murderers.

(III, 5, 11-24)

But this is no more than the Princess and her retinue do to the retarded Petrarchans of *Love's Labour's Lost*—and the lesson is presented as a highly laudable operation in that play. Phebe voices the antiromantic viewpoint so necessary to the play; and she administers a well-deserved beating to a ninny who, it seems, thrives on the diet. Why, then, the excited interruption of Rosalind, "And why, I pray you?" followed by thirty-odd lines of vulgar abuse (III, 5, 35-63) which assert the simple point that Phebe's looks are not so stellar, at that?

Because Rosalind's diatribe—a disgrace to a lady, however salutary it may be for Phebe—is again the equivalent of "touché." Phebe is a minor antiromantic voice; Rosalind is the major. Phebe is a domineering woman who, reversing the sexual roles, has mastered her man; so is Rosalind. And, subtlest, Silvius appears before Rosalind as a rather poor creature; so, therefore, does Orlando. (What does Orlando say in the final scene when confronted with the news that his wife-to-be has been

making a fool of him?) And Rosalind's response in crying up Silvius is in effect to cry up Orlando: "Down on
your knees,/And thank heaven, fasting, for a good man's
love." (III, 5, 57-58)

Rosalind's part, in general, is one that affords consistent possibilities of an antiromantic interpretation in
keeping with the open-ended invitation extended by the
play's title. She can perfectly well be played à la Angela
Brazil; equally, one can seize on the clues of her opening
lines. She enters not so much depressed as morose; and
her complaint is "the condition of my estate." (I, 2, 13-
14) In other words, a diminution of social status and
power. She cannot "forget a banished father" (I, 2, 4),
but these ambivalent words can include a sense of personal loss, and a sense of being thrust unjustly into the
shadows at Court. When she does meet her father, her
impulse is not to fall upon his bosom, but to retain her
independence and secret identity:

> I met the Duke yesterday and had much question
> with him. He asked me of what parentage I was. I
> told him, of as good as he; so he laughed and let
> me go. But what talk we of fathers when there is
> such a man as Orlando?
>
> (III, 4, 31-35)

We are entitled to draw the perfectly obvious conclusion, well borne out by her conduct throughout the play.
Rosalind misses not her father, but the status his presence
conferred; and she is motivated above all by a will to
dominate. For all Rosalind's brilliance, the generous
Celia, one of life's givers, is an implied comment on her
that one returns to.

184

An important category of relationship, then, is represented by Oliver, Duke Frederick, Jacques, and Rosalind. Each of them gives convincing testimony of being disturbed by the presence of certain others. The common element of disturbance is this: the other parallels self, and therefore subtly threatens self.

II

I now turn to a simple and obvious category, those relationships characterized by a direct clash of values. There are two such: Rosalind-Jacques, and Orlando-Jacques. They supply variations on the theme of romance challenged by antiromance. The matter is initiated theatrically when Orlando bursts into the clearing, resolved to commit some high deed in the name of a meal for Adam, and with sword bared cries "Forbear, and eat no more." (II, 7, 88) Jacques' retort (anticipating Alice's at the Mad Hatter's Tea-Party) is a classic deflation of romantic posturing: "Why, I have eat none yet." Soon the key word in such a clash, "reason," makes itself heard: Jacques' "An you will not be answered with reason, I must die." (II, 7, 100-101) This, coupled with the imperturbable good manners of the Duke, makes Orlando look a fool.

That he is conscious of this is implicit in his later exchange with Jacques, which redresses the balance of debating advantage. It is the only occasion in the play when Orlando exhibits any venom; he draws on his considerable reserves of intelligence to best Jacques. The issue between them is formalized into their parting shots: "Farewell, good Signior Love. . . . Adieu, good Monsieur

Melancholy." (III, 2, 278-281) Each, for the other, is an affected fool. But this is open contention: Jacques and Orlando bicker because they are quite unlike each other, not because they shadow each other.

The argument is carried on into the clash between Jacques and Rosalind in IV, 1. This is a shrewder debate. Rosalind (in her persona of the antiromantic Ganymede) opposes to melancholy not the open assertion of love, but the scrutiny of the realist. She asks, what good comes of melancholy? What are its benefits? And she fastens on to Jacques' lame answer of "experience" with "And your experience makes you sad. I had rather have a fool to make me merry than experience to make me sad." (IV, 1, 24-26) Here again the confrontation is open; it is sterility versus the life force.

The passages in *As You Like It* which oppose Rosalind and Orlando with Jacques are central, but could not be expanded without making the play simpler and duller. The open clash of temperament and attitude lends itself to the debate principle, but would if extended speedily lose hold upon the audience. It is the essential principle of *Love's Labour's Lost*—debate between two clearly defined camps—and one that Shakespeare never repeats in such simple form. The debate emphasis within *As You Like It* is shifted on to the brilliant device of making Rosalind a dual figure, *pour et contre*, a resort in which the conventional stage device takes over and assimilates a profound structural role. Rosalind/Ganymede *is* the debate: Rosalind/Ganymede *is* the "other" expressing self. And it merges into the conflict of personality and attitude that does not express itself in

186

such overt terms as "love" and "melancholy." Harold Jenkins' statement of "the play's principle of countering one view with another . . . the readjustment of the point of view"[3] goes far toward explaining the technique of *As You Like It*. But references to "attitude," "point of view," "values" leave out of account the remorseless personal struggles through which these agreeable abstractions are presented. And the focus for these struggles—the core of the debate, the conflict—is Touchstone.

III

John Dover Wilson is, I believe, entirely right in according Touchstone's name a symbolic significance. "As his name implies, he *tests* all that the world takes for gold, especially the gold of the golden world of pastoralism."[4] His realism, or even "materialism,"[5] is a touchstone to keep the balance of the play. We can agree that Touchstone supplies an essential ingredient in the play's composition, and that his comments—pungent, witty, realistic—on the Court, Arden, and love provide a welcome leavening. I would, however, go further than this, and assert that Touchstone in his relationships advances a standard by which we are invited to measure the other relationships in the play.

The point about Touchstone is that he has no equals. He moves in a world in which there are superiors, and inferiors; he makes this categorization in all cases, and

[3] Harold Jenkins, *"As You Like It," Shakespeare Survey 8* (Cambridge, 1955), p. 49.

[4] John Dover Wilson, *Shakespeare's Happy Comedies* (London, 1962), p. 156.

[5] *Ibid.*, p. 158.

leaves his inferiors in no doubt whatever about their status. He appears first at Court, a supple entertainer making himself agreeable to the young ladies. Even so, a reference to Duke Frederick calls forth a warning in none too gentle terms from Celia: "Speak no more of him; you'll be whipp'd for taxation one of these days." (i, 2, 78-79) Touchstone's response: "The more pity that fools may not speak wisely what wise men do foolishly" (i, 2, 80-81), and his sardonic commentary on Le Beau's scale of values establish his true credentials. This is a man of intelligence and insight, under no illusions about the Court—or Arden, for that matter. We should, therefore, receive with skepticism Jacques' account of his meeting with him. Touchstone, clearly, has been playing up to Jacques' evident assumption that a fool is a fool; or simply overacting, to take in an amateur of the trade.

Touchstone develops in Arden; the man grows before our eyes. Each of the locals encounters a Touchstone determined to enforce his moral (if not social) superiority. His entry into local society immediately signalizes this fact:

Touchstone: Holla, you clown!
Rosalind: Peace, fool! he's not thy kinsman.
Corin: Who calls?
Touchstone: Your betters, sir.

(ii, 4, 61-63)

This is an unequivocal sketch of a situation to be repeated several times later. In iii, 2 Touchstone is seen at greater leisure and he takes on the task of putting Corin in his place. Their discussion is interesting because it is a

188

clear instance of the power struggle (on Touchstone's side). Basically they are men of the same stamp, realists. Shakespeare's clowns and fools invariably are. They have, therefore, nothing really to argue about, except Humpty Dumpty's question: who is to be top? Corin's exposé of "properties" (III, 2, 22-29) has a hard common sense that Touchstone has no desire to attack frontally: "Such a one is a natural philosopher." (III, 2, 30) So he shifts his ground, and wins his battle through verbal quibbles. It is a contest of wit that Touchstone easily wins, not a true contest of values.

There are direct echoes of this scene. The unfortunate William finds Touchstone in a terrible mood, and his cadenza on the means whereby William is to be destroyed (v, 1, 45-55) effectively exposes William's pretensions to the hand of Audrey. It is a complete demolition of an inferior. Again, the penultimate scene—almost a mere excuse for a song—finds Shakespeare shading in his point. Touchstone never misses a chance to patronize whom he can; so the pages, for their pains, receive "Truly, young gentlemen, though there was no great matter in the ditty, yet the note was very untuneable. . . . I count it but time lost to hear such a foolish song." (v, 3, 33-39) We cannot speak of the "real" Touchstone emerging only when his masters are absent; but it is certainly true that the Duke, before whom Touchstone displays his set pieces (v, 4) so skillfully, sees only a part of the man.

Touchstone must, however, be judged principally on his relations with Audrey and Jacques. The contributory evidence, which I have just cited, is necessary to estab-

189

lish the bent of his mind and the true facts of his relationships. These are demonstrated chiefly in III, 3. Audrey and Touchstone have already come to an understanding: "And how, Audrey, am I the man yet? Doth my simple feature content you?" (III, 3, 2-3)—and it is plain that Touchstone's simple feature does. Now why does a man of Touchstone's stamp single out Audrey for a permanent liaison? Critics, suspecting the worst, have rushed in with their explanations. For Helen Gardner, "Touchstone's marriage to Audrey is a mere coupling."[6] For Harold Jenkins, it is the "animal lust which propels him towards Audrey."[7] James Smith's extraordinary view of Touchstone's drives is: "Touchstone is on the way to tragedy because he has allowed desire to get out of control."[8] Sex, the consensus asserts, is certainly at the bottom of it. But there are some caveats to be lodged. First, Touchstone is a character who is stated, not explained. We have no formal means of opening up his mind; he has no soliloquies, is never on stage alone. Second, sex is quite unsatisfactory as the sole motive for Touchstone's marriage. The Audreys of this world do not demand a price; the Audrey of this play does not ask it. She is perfectly ready to be married by a hedge-priest: "Faith, the priest was good enough, for all the old gentleman's saying." (v, 1, 3-4) The critics who pounce on Touchstone for his bottomless cynicism in considering an illegal marriage to Audrey—so that he can leave her thereafter—customarily omit to add a detail of some consequence: Touchstone does, in fact, marry Audrey perfectly properly. He

[6] Gardner, *op.cit.*, p. 68.   [7] Jenkins, *op.cit.*, p. 49.
[8] James Smith, *"As You Like It," Scrutiny* VII (1940), 31-32.

insists on it. Audrey is well satisfied with something less, but it is Touchstone who resists her: "We shall find a time, Audrey. Patience, gentle Audrey." (v, 1, 1-2) It is, as usual, necessary to pay attention to what people do as well as what they say. Touchstone would have had a better Press had he taken over some of Orlando's cast-off sentiments to clothe his "coupling."

But the question of motivation remains. We can only take Touchstone's action at face value, the ironic acceptance of a slut by a man who will always be her superior. In the context of Touchstone's other relationships, it is a likely guess that the certainty that he will remain the dominant partner is uppermost in his mind. He undoubtedly likes to demonstrate his mastery in a series of brisk imperatives: "Come, sweet Audrey" (iii, 3, 83); "Patience, gentle Audrey" (v, 1, 1-2); "Trip, Audrey! trip, Audrey!" (v, 1, 60); "Come, Audrey" (v, 3, 40); "Bear your body more seeming, Audrey" (v, 4, 65-66). The dulcet adjectives fade before the end; she is an object to be possessed. Doubtless sex enters into the matter—this is customarily so with marriages, even those of Silvius, Oliver, and Orlando—but to accept it as the sole motive is to take Touchstone at his own word (precisely what he wishes the company to do) and to ignore the gap between the word and action. The version that Touchstone presents to the Duke is a double bluff that obliquely but justly indicates the truth of the matter: "A poor virgin, sir, an ill-favored thing, sir, *but mine own.*" (v, 4, 55-56)

Still, the matter is entangled with Jacques' presence, and the Jacques-Touchstone relationship must now be

191

reopened. Jacques, I have suggested, is both envious and disdainful of the fool that caricatures him. Touchstone, for his part, is wary of a social superior who patronizes him insufferably but might put in a good word for him with the authorities (as Jacques does, in the final scene). It is, of course, quite misleading to allude to Touchstone and Jacques as "usually allies."[9] Theirs is the tension between amateur and professional, with a social gulf unconfirmed by the allocation of talent. The confrontation takes place in III, 3, Jacques discovering himself as Audrey and Touchstone are about to make use of Sir Oliver's irregular services. Touchstone is caught at a disadvantage but rallies well:

> Good even, good Master What-ye-call't. How do you, sir? You are very well met. Goddild you for your last company; I am very glad to see you. Even a toy in hand here, sir. Nay, pray be covered.
>
> (III, 3, 63-67)

This is a brave attempt at counterpatronage. Jacques instantly reminds Touchstone of his social function and status: "Will you be married, *motley*?" (III, 3, 68) And Touchstone parries the sneer with an apparently complacent account of man and his desires:

> As the ox hath his bow, sir, the horse his curb, and the falcon her bells, so man hath his desires; and as pigeons bill, so wedlock would be nibbling.
>
> (III, 3, 69-71)

[9] *Ibid.*, p. 26.

When, however, Jacques turns the knife again—"And will you, *being a man of your breeding*, be married under a bush, like a beggar?" (III, 3, 89-91)—Touchstone advances the crux by which we are to judge him:

> I am not in the mind but I were better to be married of him than of another; for he is not like to marry me well; and not being well married, it will be a good excuse for me hereafter to leave my wife.
>
> (III, 3, 78-81)

Now this speech is normally rendered as an "aside" by modern editors. It is not so indicated in the Folio (which is, of course, not given to stage directions) and the relegation of the speech to "aside" status is pure editorial conjecture. I contend that we have no reason for accepting the conjecture. There is no soliloquy of Touchstone's elsewhere; there is no other reasonable opportunity for an aside, or parenthetic soliloquy.[10] This is a character designed to be presented solely in terms of dialogue. The speech makes excellent sense if it is regarded as whispered to Jacques; in which case it becomes a pseudo-motive, a piece of man-of-the-world's cynicism put up to protect the gap in Touchstone's armor against the sneers of Jacques. He *must* defend himself. Touchstone has no intention, however, of allowing Jacques a permanent

---

[10] I take it as indicative of Shakespeare's overall concept of *As You Like It* that there are virtually no soliloquies save for Oliver, whose hatred is technically indispensable yet requiring internal explanation. There are, therefore, very few points that are psychologically "fixed." This is a play exceptionally open to diversity of interpretation.

sneer at his subwedding; so after the face saving formula of "a flaw in the procedure may be useful later" he allows himself to be persuaded into a proper wedding. Touchstone is a much cleverer fellow than Jacques. No one ever knows when *he* is hit. Nor could we even guess it, without reviewing the whole pattern of his behavior.

Touchstone, then, belongs to the type of character portrayal that (since Bradley's day) has come to be recognized as a Shakespearian crux, located classically in the problem of Iago.[11] That is, he compels us to look for motives that are not stated in the text, which does however contain part-motives or pseudo-motives. I find the missing motive here to be the drive to power, because that is of a piece with Touchstone's relationships with his un-superiors; and because it embodies the drift of the whole play.

Touchstone, in fact, is the reduction of the ideas latent in *As You Like It.* He exhibits in gross form the will to mastery that is discernible in the actions of his betters. The play is set into a formal framework of political struggle, the usurpation of Duke Frederick; it focuses on the mating dance of a masterful female round her captive male, "my child's father" as Rosalind herself elegantly epitomizes him (I, 3, 11); it presents a running debate, ostensibly on values, in effect to protect the egos of the debaters; it etches in relationships with a controlled quantum of acid. The latent motivation of the characters is an impulse to protect themselves against the psychological threats from without. And this accounts for the

[11] A. C. Bradley, *Shakespearean Tragedy* (London, 1957), pp. 181-190.

sudden conversions of Duke Frederick and Oliver, who have earlier given indications that Duke Senior and Orlando represent threats to their psyches, not their persons. Of the others, Jacques finds intolerable the presence of Duke Senior and Touchstone, because *he* caricatures them. Rosalind finds Phebe's behavior to Silvius an affront, for the same reason. Even the gentle Orlando has a flash of an intolerable presence: "But, O, how bitter a thing it is to look into happiness through another man's eyes!" (v, 2, 41-42) Virtually all the relationships manifest a sense of unease, of latent or open hostility. There is little true accord in Arden, prior to the final scene; and the audience is entitled, if it wishes, to its reservations even then. The idyll of Arden is an idea as much under fire as the denizens of the forest; and the final path that leads away from forest to Court is a change of milieu, not a way out of those problems.

CHAPTER X

The Messages of *Twelfth Night*

The main view of *Twelfth Night* is not in doubt. The comedy is a conclusive, magisterial exposition of techniques and tonalities; it recapitulates and restates the themes that have engaged its author since *The Comedy of Errors*. It is a terminus of evolution, a work whose concerns and mastery openly prohibit a successor. Yet the direction, or thrust of the play remains in dispute. The title nicely catches the ambivalence of the matter. *Twelfth Night* is a feast, and an end to feasting. It implies a sour awareness that the real winter is to come. The balance, the implied apprehension of the matter sort well with an author at the mid-point of his career, and at the mid-point of his Biblical span. So the symbolism of the title, confirmed in the explicit invitation of the subtitle, offers a choice of interpretation. And this invitation has led to a divergence of response. Very broadly, two major responses to *Twelfth Night* may be discerned. The one is impressed, above all, with the final situation of Malvolio, and by the irreconcilable element in the comic structure that he represents. This view may run to such extremes as the *Malvolio, A Tragedy* title attributed to Charles I. The other view, currently much more fashionable, sees the comedy in the tradition of social corrective. The supporters of this view experience small sympathy for Malvolio,[1] are impressed by the tenuous resemblances between Sir Toby and the Lord of Misrule,[2] and are perfectly content with the pairings that

[1] Indeed, they rigorously suppress what sympathy they have.

"Malvolio, of course, is justly punished. He has earned his mad scene, and with the aid of Feste he has made it comic. As a result of his humiliation he has also earned some sort of redress. Yet he is ridiculous in his arrogance to the end, and his threatened revenge, now that he is powerless to effect it, sustains the comedy and the characterization and prevents the obtrusion of destructive pathos." Joseph H. Summers, "The Masks of *Twelfh Night*," in *The University Review*, XXII (1955), p. 30.

"Most people now agree that Charles Lamb's sympathy for the steward's enterprise and commiseration for his sorrows is a romantic and bourgeois distortion. . . . [He is] a kind of foreign body, to be expelled by laughter, in Shakespeare's free-and-easy comedy." C. L. Barber, *Shakespeare's Festive Comedy* (Princeton, 1959), pp. 255-256, 257.

[2] "Sir Toby is gentlemanly liberty incarnate, a specialist in it. He lives at ease, enjoying heritage, the something-for-nothing which this play celebrates. . . . He is like Falstaff in maintaining saturnalian paradox and in playing impromptu the role of lord of misrule. But in his whole relation to the world he is fundamentally different from Prince Hal's great buffoon. Falstaff makes a career of misrule; Sir Toby uses misrule to show up a careerist." Barber, *op.cit.*, pp. 250, 251.

This is an extraordinarily tendentious account of the matter. Lords of misrule are licensed by the authorities; Sir Toby is warned several times by Olivia, not just by Malvolio. "Gentlemanly liberty incarnate" against "careerism" is a false opposition. One might as accurately speak of parasitism against ambition. The play depicts both Sir Toby and Malvolio with entire detachment, but while there are moments when one can respect if not like Malvolio, there is no point at which Sir Toby can command either response. For that, one requires more than a telling rejoinder in favor of cakes and ale. The drunken venom of Sir Toby's final words completes our picture of the man; and it is not one that merges happily with the lord of misrule.

close the play.[3] One ought at once to declare one's sympathies in this necessarily continuing cleavage of opinion. Certainly one can say that ambivalence is the essence of *Twelfth Night*, that the play leaves on record an equilibrium rather than a judgment. But this is only to postpone a verdict on the point of equilibrium. My inclination is toward the first view; I think the ironic and somber elements in *Twelfth Night* more important than is commonly granted.

And this is not only for reasons confined to the text of *Twelfth Night*. That play concludes a smaller, as well as a larger movement of the comedies. *Twelfth Night* is the culmination of the wave that throws forward *The Merchant of Venice*, and that follows up with *Much Ado About Nothing* and *As You Like It*. These four comedies seem to contribute as a group to Shakespeare's develop-

---

[3] "Content" is too mild of the extreme cases, some of which I quote. Porter Williams writes of an ending in which "Virtue, open-heartedness, and sense have prevailed." Porter Williams, Jr., "Mistakes in *Twelfth Night* and Their Resolution: A Study in Some Relationships of Plot and Theme," *PMLA*, LXXVI (1961), 193-199.

Joseph Summers sees "a vision of delight upon delight, in which lovers have neither to wear nor to penetrate disguises since they are at last invulnerable to error and laughter." Summers, *op.cit.*, p. 30.

Peter G. Phialas overbids this in his celebration of a conclusion that "projects a vision of the lovers' ideal," and of "a simple conception of the way to happiness, namely through individual as well as communal integration." Peter G. Phialas, *Shakespeare's Romantic Comedies* (Chapel Hill, North Carolina, 1966), pp. 280, 277.

A definition of "communal integration" that includes Malvolio, and of "lovers' ideal" that covers the mating methods of Olivia and Orsino (to say nothing of their complaisant partners) is somewhat too wide to be critically useful.

ment over this period. If we knew no more of *Twelfth Night* than that it followed hard upon the other three, we should be skeptical of a judgment that celebrates the play's "communal integration," that accepts "love" as a word absolutely validating all transactions carried out in its name, and that assumes that the comedy takes Sir Toby's side against Malvolio.

I

The main business of *Twelfth Night* is illusion, error, and deceit. Error is a matter of plot alone, stemming from the chance of mistaken identity. But illusion and deceit are inherent to the main actors. The play can usefully be analyzed in terms of fantasy (or illusion) and reality; and its action I take to be founded on the series of messages which run through all five Acts.

We can begin by classifying the principals. Orsino is a fantasist, and music is the symbol of his fantasy. His vein is auto-erotic, clear from the opening line, and in his curtain line, "Love-thoughts lie rich when canopied with bow'rs." (I, 1, 42) His credo is "So full of shapes is fancy/That it alone is high fantastical." (I, 1, 14-15) The symbol, and not the thing itself, is what Orsino requires. It is *simpliste* to speak of him as being prey to illusions. For Orsino, illusion is the only reality. He is contrasted with Viola, who is a reality figure. Her first words, "What country, friends, is this?" (I, 2, 1) ask a question about the nature of reality, whereas Orsino's had stated a demand for the status quo of fantasy. Her appraisal of the Captain (I, 2, 47-51) confirms her capacity to distinguish between appearance and reality, and music

199

for her becomes a vocation and employment, not a fantasy symbol. Significantly, she makes of it a mode of communication: "For I can sing,/And speak to him in many sorts of music." (I, 2, 57-58)

Olivia is in part under the sway of illusion, but is more poseuse than fantasist. When we first meet her, her self-chosen role of grief-prostrated sister is clearly becoming irksome. She is ready to be delivered from her ennui by the clown; and his catechism establishes the folly of her over-long mourning. Nevertheless, her colloquy with Viola reveals her intelligence and capacity to lay aside her pose. In the course of their meeting (I, 5) she symbolically unveils herself, and changes (with Viola) from prose, in this scene the language of fencing and social deception, to verse, the language of truth and intensely felt emotion. Viola thus elicits from Olivia the communication of truth: "Your lord does know my mind; I cannot love him. . . ./He might have took his answer long ago." (I, 5, 243, 249) That is the truth, for Olivia and Orsino. But the element of fantasy in Olivia's mind is now fixed upon Viola, and her "fivefold blazon." (I, 5, 279) Olivia's words are prophetic: "I do I know not what, and fear to find/Mine eye too great a flatterer for my mind." (I, 5, 294-295)

Deception is a mechanism of illusion, and Sir Toby is an agent of the world of illusions—until the realities combine to break his head, and marry him off to Maria (and good luck, too, most of us feel). Sir Andrew, the deceived, has a taste for illusion: "I delight in masques and revels sometimes altogether" (I, 3, 101-102), which must coexist with occasional inklings of the truth: "Methinks sometimes I have no more wit than a Christian or an ordinary man has." (I, 3, 76-77) He shares with his mentor a taste for music, and wine, whereby the realities of existence can be transmuted. With their aid, the mortality of the "four elements" can be resisted, and the truth that "what's to come is still unsure" rendered bearable. Yet these are trustless solaces; music angers the authorities, and Sir Andrew is probably right that had not Sir Toby been in drink, he would have tickled Sebastian othergates than he did. (V, 1, 184-186) But generally—and this includes Fabian and perhaps Maria too—the play makes the point that deception is a dangerous business, apt to backfire. The world of illusion is not one for easy meddling.

There remain Malvolio and the clown. Malvolio, for all his undoubted intelligence and ability, has a dangerous fantasy. His error is a conceited and subjective interpretation of data, which confirms instead of challenging his fantasy—that he will follow in the path of the Yeoman of the Wardrobe. Malvolio's dream, at its height, attains a quintessential denial of reality: "I discard you" (III, 4, 83), which anticipates Coriolanus' "I banish you." He presents most forcibly the situation of several characters in the play, that of the man held spellbound by the power of illusion. Malvolio's opposite and adversary is Feste, the clown. He, in the design of *Twelfth Night*, is the reality figure, and the mediator of reality. "I wear not motley in my brain." (I, 5, 51-52) His operations relate to both worlds, for he speaks truth through folly, and expresses reality through the fantasy symbol, music. His song that supplies the epilogue carries the burden of a certain reality, rain, that matches the Winter Song at the close of *Love's Labour's Lost*. Feste's skills include command of music, disguise, and words. His concern with linguistic analysis is especially significant, and he has the philosopher's preoccupation with words, the symbolic tools for grappling with truth. Thus his discussion with Viola (III, 1) of words as lies: "A sentence is but a chev'ril glove to a good wit. How quickly the wrong side may be turned outward!" (III, 1, 11-13) Thus his penchant for conceptualizing reality, "Nothing that is so is so" (IV, 1, 8), and the central statement in the following scene:

> for, as the old hermit of Prague, that never saw pen and ink, very wittily said to a niece of King Gorboduc, "That that is is"; so, I, being Master Parson, am Master Parson; for what is "that" but that, and "is" but is?
>
> (IV, 2, 12-16)

This, apart from being perhaps the clearest statement in the canon of the very Shakespearean idea of being-as-role playing, asserts the particular concern of this play, that illusion may create its own reality. The least deceived of all men, Feste's view of the principals—from the early catechism of Olivia onwards—is totally without illusion. As chorus he mediates between the two worlds of fantasy and reality.

II

The reality of the action presented to us is repeatedly questioned, through means which range from the mate-

rial and evident to the subtle and conceptual. Nothing
need be said of the disguise of Viola, the confusions between Viola and Sebastian, and the deceptions engineered by Sir Toby and his followers. These are merely
the physical manifestations of the action. But these
events promote a sense of paradox and equivocation that
is heightened by certain passages in the dialogue. Thus,
there are the paradoxes of the Viola-Olivia exchange:

Olivia: Stay.
      I prithee tell me what thou think'st of me.
Viola: That you do think you are not what you are.
Olivia: If I think so, I think the same of you.
Viola: Then think you right. I am not what I am.
Olivia: I would you were as I would have you be.
Viola: Would it be better, madam, than I am?
      I wish it might, for now I am your fool.

(III, 1, 134-141)

Viola's last word takes up one of the central paradoxes
of the play, that of wisdom in folly, folly in wisdom. To
express it seems one of Feste's prime functions. Again,
Feste's fascination with the antitheses of appearance and
reality is codified in the passages already quoted: III, 1,
11-13; IV, 1, 8; IV, 2, 12-16. And these passages find an
echo in Orsino's reaction to physical similarities: "A
natural perspective that is and is not." (V, 1, 209)

Such paradoxes and equivocations yield up subtler
questions concerning the conduct of the principals, and
hence the nature of sexual love itself. The passion of
Orsino, as we have seen, is highly ambivalent. It comprehends his taste for a girl-like boy—or is it a girl remi-

niscent of a boy? Or a girl, reminiscent of a boy who was a girl in disguise, played in any event by a boy. . . . The regressions are baffling, and we cannot stop them at any one phase, and say with certitude, "*this* is the key to Orsino." Similarly, the outrageous substitution of Sebastian for Cesario—the news of which is received with silence and assent by Olivia—raises unanswerable questions concerning her psychology. Which, of Sebastian and Cesario, one asks, constitutes the proper objective of Olivia's desires? And which is the substitute?

These questions are not stilled by the terms in which Orsino and Olivia account for their behavior. Olivia speaks of "A most extracting frenzy of mine own" (v, 1, 273); but she can hardly, at that stage of events, do other than to seek to distance herself from an absurdity of passion. It is not clear why her marriage with Sebastian falls into a totally different category. On Orsino's part, there is the equivocation of "love" and "fancy." This, of course, is the vibration of the opening speech, which begins "If music be the food of love," continues with "O spirit of love," and concludes "So full of shapes is fancy/ That it alone is high fantastical." (I, 1, 1-15) The last two lines constitute a tribute, it seems, to the power of the imagination in creating its own structures. This shift from "love" to "fancy" is quite inadequately recognized in those editions, and they are legion, which provide a simple footnote at line 14: "*fancy*, love." In fact, the *Oxford English Dictionary* does not mention "love" until sense 8b of "fancy." The premier senses stress the associations of caprice, fantasy, whim, and so on. "Fancy" extends the idea of the fragility of male passion, a con-

204

tinual concern of the comedies from *The Two Gentle-men of Verona* onwards. In view of Orsino's penultimate word in the play, one can hardly regard the issue as resolved. In sum, then, there can be little doubt concerning the motivations of Viola and Sebastian; but Orsino and Olivia remain, at the conclusion, in a situation of suspended ambivalence.

III

The burden of the theme of fantasy and reality is entrusted to a particular device: the message. The action of *Twelfth Night* is in great part the business, literal and symbolic, of communication. Each Act sees one or more formal messages—I do not count informal and oral bringing of news. They constitute the archetypal action of the play.

The first scene contains an important message: Olivia to Orsino, a declaration of her absurd vow to mourn her brother for seven years. It is not a true communication, merely the publication of a fantasy; the "message" is a self-to-self statement. The same is true of Orsino's reply to Viola (I, 4); he, too, is announcing his own fantasy: "Surprise her with discourse of my dear faith;/It shall become thee well to act my woes." (I, 4, 24-25) The resonance of "act" is suggestive. Still, the nuncio's function is faithfully carried out by Viola:

I will on with my speech in your praise and then show you the heart of my message. . . . Tell me your mind. I am a messenger.

(I, 5, 181-2 . . . 194-5)

205

Viola has the understanding and intelligence for the discharge of her office. Even so, Olivia and Orsino cannot be said to communicate. The matter is repeated with greater emphasis and clarity in II, 4, when Orsino again sends his declaration of love. He is simply not interested in any answer but acceptance.

Viola: But if she cannot love you, sir?
Duke: I cannot be so answered.

(II, 4, 86-87)

In other words, he will not accept the realities of the situation. It is a manifesto of noncommunication. Olivia's message to Viola (II, 2) is no more satisfactory. The messenger, Malvolio, has no idea of what is going on, but Viola immediately apprehends the situation: "She loves me sure." (II, 2, 21) The fault lies in the sender, prey to another species of illusion.

The play's main pseudo-message is the letter, supposedly from Olivia to Malvolio. His fantasy has been penetrated, and the "message" is no more than an inflation of his hopes. The scene in which Malvolio discovers the letter is, in addition to its other qualities, pure symbolist drama. The point is that Malvolio goes for a walk in the sun.

Maria: He has been yonder i'the sun practicing behavior to his own shadow this half hour.

(II, 5, 14-15)

And "sun," in the terms of this play, is the associate of folly. Feste makes the connection, to Viola: "Foolery, sir, does walk about the orb like the sun; it shines every-

where." (III, 1, 37-38) The connection is in any case
confirmed by IV, 2 (the structural balance to II, 5, in the
design of *Twelfth Night*), which presents the complementary paradox of reason in darkness. So Malvolio's
journey into illusion takes the form of a walk in the sun.

Thus the comic business develops the serious concern
of *Twelfth Night*, the fallibility of human communication. And the variations on this theme continue in Act III,
through Sir Andrew's letter to Viola/Cesario. That letter
is totally misconceived, a triumph of noncommunication.
Sir Andrew has misjudged the situation, the identity of
his addressee, his language—and to crown all, his message is not even delivered. His effort ranks wtih Malvolio's as the non-message of the play. Sir Toby (whose
role now contrasts with Viola, the ideal messenger)
delivers orally two lying messages, to Viola and Sir
Andrew. Their purpose is merely deception. But Sir
Toby's view of the essence of correspondence has already
been made plain in his advice to Sir Andrew in III, 2:
the key word is "lies." (III, 2, 40)

That is as far as *Twelfth Night* can go in its variations
on failure of communication. The remainder of the play
shows a struggling toward the light. Act IV, 2 is the critical scene. It reveals a Malvolio purged of fantasy, and
striving only to make contact with the realities of the
world. Matched with the sunfilled garden of II, 5, the cell
completes the pairing of symbolist scenes. The darkness
that figures ignorance—a form of illusion—closes about
Malvolio, but his mind is clear:

Malvolio: I am not mad, Sir Topas. I say to you this
house is dark.

207

Clown: Madman, thou errest. I say there is no darkness but ignorance, in which thou art more
puzzled than the Egyptians in their fog.

Malvolio: I say this house is as dark as ignorance,
though ignorance were as dark as hell; and
I say there was never man thus abused. I am
no more mad than you are. Make the trial of
it in any constant question.

(IV, 2, 40-48)

Malvolio's attempts to penetrate the darkness are ob-
structed by the clown's feignings. But Malvolio has re-
gained a human dignity, that of a man as disciplined
guardian of his faculties. His language is controlled and
just: "I think nobly of the soul and in no way approve
his opinion." (IV, 2, 54-55) And he has, at last, a full
grasp of the priorities of human needs. "Good fool, some
ink, paper, and light; and convey what I will set down
to my lady." (IV, 2, 106-108) The light of reason, a
just message to compose, and the means of communication, he can command. The clown cannot refuse his
cooperation.

And this message, from Malvolio to Olivia, is the
apotheosis of the final Act. It is the message of a man in
full possession of his senses and the situation; it is mediated, not by the clown (his tone, as he himself seems to
feel, would be wrong) but by the nondescript and "neu-
tral" Fabian; it finds an understanding audience, both the
Duke ("This savors not much of distraction," V, 1, 304)
and Olivia, "He hath been most notoriously abused."

(v, 1, 368) Malvolio's letter has the distinction of be-ing—of all the formal messages in *Twelfth Night*—the only true communication. It is the only occasion in the play when the human mind, unencumbered by fantasy, reaches out toward another human mind and finds its message fairly delivered, understandingly received, and answered. All the other messages are deceptions or self-illusions.

The principals, however, are not compelled to face reality in the same way as Malvolio. Orsino, the premier fantasist, merely switches faces in his image of the dream-woman. His first impulse on learning of Viola's sex is "let me see thee in thy woman's weeds" (v, 1, 265); and the unabashed auto-eroticism of his humor is underscored in his final words to Viola: "But when in other habits you are seen,/Orsino's mistress and his fancy's queen." (v, 1, 376-377) For "fancy," read "fan-tasy." His last line is a poised, ambiguous phrase. Will Viola control his fantasy, or embody it? One cannot prophesy. Olivia, too, is doubtless well off with the sensi-ble Sebastian, but the "most extracting frenzy of mine own" (v, 1, 273) testifies to her susceptibility to the caprice of passion. As for the others, Sir Andrew's fan-tasy is ended. He had rather than forty pound he were at home; the phrase is a calculated multiplication of his earlier desire to exchange forty shillings for the trappings of folly. (ii, 3, 18-19) His anagnorisis is to hear the truth from Sir Toby: "Will *you* help? An ass-head and a cox-comb and a knave, a thin-faced knave, a gull?" (v, 1, 198-199) We do not know his reactions; the audience will be able to savor his horrified face; but that truth, as with others in the play, must continue to fester. Sir Toby himself has married Maria "In recompense thereof . . ." (v, 1, 354), and in view of Maria's talents and shrewishness one is inclined to regard "recompense" as a pregnant word.

And there remains Malvolio. Here, I think, the critics have overcompensated. We have been told with considerable frequency of late years that one ought not to feel at all sorry for him, that he deserved all he got, that Elizabethan audiences would have laughed at his final disgrace, and that compassion is a nineteenth century invention anyway. No doubt all this is true. Elizabethan audiences, like modern ones, can never have been lacking in those who find only the most exquisite humor in the final "I'll be revenged on the whole pack of you." But I don't think it really matters whether one feels sorry for Malvolio, or not. The point, surely, is that he is *there*. Malvolio is an unassimilable element, a part of what is conceived to be the structure of comedy, that refuses to participate in the final dance. That dance is a gavotte of the realists coolly taking on the fantasists; it is scarcely the "communal integration" of the sentimentalists. The "golden time" that Orsino speaks of sounds hollowly.

The play as a whole is a masterly exposition of theme through device, that is to say of form. If we agree that the theme of *Twelfth Night* is reality and illusion, then this theme, obviously, is expressed through disguise, deception, and error. But the action of *Twelfth Night*, as I have shown, consists of a succession of pseudo-messages, products of the world of illusion. And it incorporates two scenes of startling theater, in which Malvolio receives, and sends, a message. At these points, the scenes of sunlight and of darkness, the symbolism of the drama becomes overt. Yet they are only the most compelling manifestation of an action that, in Shakespeare's way, is always reaching toward symbolism. The literal events generate their further meanings.

The form of *Twelfth Night*, as I maintain, should govern our interpretation. The open-ended invitation of the subtitle is no reason for disregarding the structure of the play. Its atmosphere one can in part ascribe to a particular production, and this will vary very greatly. Yet I think W. H. Auden is right to sense the "inverted commas around the 'fun.' "[4] This stems from the nature of the action, and the questions left in the air concerning the principals. Exposure to reality has, in different ways, involved pain for the "comic" characters; Sir Toby, Sir Andrew, and Malvolio. But for Orsino and Olivia, the ending is illusion condoned. To speak of "unmasking"[5] is surely misleading, for they have begun neither to understand nor confront their problems; nor need they. The cynicism of *Twelfth Night* lies in its acceptance of

[4] W. H. Auden, *The Dyer's Hand* (New York, 1962), p. 520.
[5] Thus, Summers (*op.cit.*, p. 30) speaks of the "discarding of all the lovers' masks," and Porter Williams (*op.cit.*, p. 196) of Orsino and Olivia "assuming a false mask." Masks are detachable, elements of human personality not so. " 'True' identities" (Summers, *op.cit.*, p. 32) exist in no realm penetrable to human observation, and the inverted commas provide no defense for the epithet.

211

the truths that fantasy need not bring unhappiness, nor exposure to reality happiness. The preoccupation with illusion and reality, madness and sanity, wisdom and folly, points unmistakably toward *King Lear*. The synthesis of theme and device could not be repeated within the genre of comedy.

Index